Parents

DON'T OWE THEIR CHILDREN
NOTHING

Brenda Campbell

WORKBOOK PRESS LLC
187 E Warm Springs Rd,
Suite B285, Las Vegas, NV 89119, USA

Website: https://workbookpress.com/
Hotline: 1-888-818-4856
Email: admin@workbookpress.com

Ordering Information:
Quantity sales. Special discounts are available on quantity purchases by corporations, associations, and others.
For details, contact the publisher at the address above.

ISBN-13:   978-1-953839-27-5 (Paperback Version)
              978-1-953839-28-2 (Digital Version)

REV. DATE: 06/23/2022

PARENTS DON'T OWE

THEIR CHILDREN

NOTHING

By: Ms. Brenda Campbell

INTRODUCTION

This book I'm writing is about a mother who had to go through many changes with her adult girls all the disconnections as they became adults how ungrateful and how they wanted to control me. I know us children will be children until they turn eighteen years old leaving home with their lives increasingly separate lives for ours it's a challenge when parent step back we love and support them when they go through their ups and downs but if they lose their way and their faith, we as parent feel as if we have failed with adult children they need to realize that us as parent do everything for them without us as parent they wouldn't exit.

Parents are the first people who deserve their children Allenton especially if what parent have put a lot of effect and passion to protect them the parent still finds a place in them home when thing go wrong, we looked after them watched them grow made sure harm did not come their way this is the reason they should thank their parents for being there for them and supporting them into days world the kids away thinking that their parent owes them something when it is not ways have to do with material thing and money lot of time it has to do with just respecting us as parent. Parenthood is a story that never ends. In the painful moments, I could never through parenthood away I learned and grew with my children.

I've read almost every motherhood and parenthood book and not one book touched on black teenager fatherless children don't get it wrong a brief description was giving however, what these teenagers and adults go though is not brief. My book will help mother spots changes accurately asked the children and find the proper help needed for individual child. Although I have two girls if you are a parent then you will know that every child is different.so the next few pages I am going to describe the ups and down of each one of my children and what I went through with each one and their status. Throughout the years of my life and the experiences that I had in raising my children and how much it hurt after they got grown when they turned on me, I never thought that the ones that I had raised the ones that I kept under my wings all these years would done the way that I would never thought the ones that I the one who turned out to hurt me. I tried so hard to figure out what I really done to them I would ask them why what part of loving them and learning that they don't get the bottom of the line is that they let me down and scar me for life not just that my trust I had for them had went out the door now, as I began to talk about how I was able to live through all this too was able to tell my stories and the struggles after they had gotten grown being a single mother was very hard as I tell long hard story and the bad experiences that I had in raising them and them being rude ungrateful disrespectful and still survive in keeping my head up and keep focusing on and keeping my mind on GOD.

It was a challenge for me as a mother to go through sweet loving children to disrespectful rude I would never have to go through all these problems and trying to be the mother that they wanted me to be but all of that changed they just wanted me to feel like them I stood by them from birth and through the days and nights hours all the times I held them nourished them feed them love them changing them and clothing them laughing encouraging giving them advise and being there with them as the go through there trials I stayed by them the whole time even though they went through what they went through I still love my children and it was a challenge for me and it was very interesting to me though it was a lot of work through the crying that I did it was very painful and all the crying that I did when I lost my son and my husband I would have thought of my children having me to continue to hurt me and keep me I thought I could lean on them in my trials and they would be able to comfort me things that I had accomplished in life I tried to share my good news with them it was away negativity they never supported me on nothing it was they was pulling and tearing me down to them it didn't work I put all my trust in them and the stabbed me in the back they treated me so s bad it was a shame the thing I wanted was a peace of mind I had so much on my mind I just had a lot to say, and I thought I could go to them and yes, I could have gone to a professional, but I was comfortable with them I did not know they would just treat me like I was no one I was the mother that birth them and this is what I got in the replace of rude and disrespect when they came to me.

I sat and listen to each problem they had I didn't have to but as a mother I wanted to because I cared, and I love them thy are my life it would be days that I would just sit in my room and think if I should keep moving on or give up, I was very depressed and miserable it was like my life was a turn oil it was like standing still at a crossroad just barely holding on like closure was already gone I didn't know what to do just looking at how the done and mistreated me and how they were trying to destroy me.

I just didn't know what to do and I just didn't know how to deal with this situation it was like I was just a movie it was like it didn't have a perfect seen until I edit out the parts that had no ending to my life it was like an no ending to a beginning the beginning played a big part, but the ending played a bigger part of my life as I continue to write my book PARENTS DON'T OWE THERE CHILDRENS NOTHING was the experience of my life of my children my youngest daughter the baby girl as her growing up she was the sweetest kindness had a good heart she was quite she looked up to her big sisters she watched everything they did as they were the oldest, she took everything in she listens and paid attention and she knew who to pray on as she got older as years went, she had started hanging out with wrong crowds it had gotten so bad if she could not get her way with me, she would do whatever she could to do to destroy me she would lie on me she would steal to support her boyfriend no matter how it hurt me she would steal my credit cards and pay her phone bill her boyfriend bills and then give the credit cards to other people she never cared just if she can pull me down the thing of it all was when I told her that after she drop out of school had her baby and decided she didn't have to go back to school she decided that she didn't have to listen to me and she could just do what she wanted to me always ask her what make you think that a parent owe you something when you messed up your own life, she said no what I do you are still obligated to do for us "who told you that".

I stated that someone has told you wrong I guess at that time Satan was talking in her ear it all started on September 18, 2015, it way the morning I got up I had a good night woke up with high hopes and ready to get my day starting my morning good had me coffee and breakfast doing my usually routine in the mother taking care of my mother which she had a stroke and then my daughter which she is bed written took care of them getting ready to get my day started cleaning and walked back-to-back room knocked on the door to ask my daughter to get my granddaughter up to get her ready to go to school didn't know she had company until I went back to the room to get the granddaughter jacket and shoes it didn't don on me to cut the lights on in the room because I knew where her thing was.

I kept on looking at the bed looked like it was a lot of pillows on the bed so I am curios, so I cut the lights on and seen she had her boyfriend in the bed I shook the young man and told him he had to get up and leave my house he just rolled over and turned his head like he didn't hear me or didn't have to go so my daughter came back in the back room and told the young man he didn't have to go anywhere she was very verbal cussing me out shouting saying all kind of nasty things her boyfriend told her to keep cussing me out and fight me if she must and he would have her back so while telling him that he had to leave I also told her she had to leave too she told me she was not going yes u are I replied to her by that time she had leaped over the couch and there was a chair I picked it up a chair and put it in front of my face to keep her from hitting me when she dives over the couch, she hit her head on the chair and split her head wide open now here come her boyfriend to try to fight me and now she is telling him to beat me up my own child and the other daughter is on the phone telling the 911 operator that I had it her.

And she seen everything which she didn't the other daughter had step outside to put grand kids on the bus the middle daughter is on the phone with 911 in saying all these negativities to the police the whole time they were plaining to get me away from the house so they could have boys over to the house to lay up now they had told the police that I lost my mind and that I was crazy. And I need to be removed from the home now to remind you that my mom is bedridden with a feeding tube and daughter is bed written also now when the officers got in the house. I was in the living room and they told me to put down what I was doing and come in the other room with my hands up they put handcuffs on me took me put me in the car they told the young man to take his clothes back in the house and I couldn't make him leave then the other came out to the car and ask me to give me all the information so she can get me out of jail.

I told her no I would just stay in there they wanted the house they wanted to control so there my mom at home no care my daughter at home no care did they care no they were having a good time then they decided to put a criminal trespass on me well I was order not to go 200 feet to my home I had to stay away from my home for 30 days all of they were afraid of me I am not going to harm no one I had time to sit and think and I just said I just threw my hands up because I just got tired, and I knew I could not win for losing I just didn't know what to do how could they turn on me I just didn't know what else to do or say I had to find another place to stay I had to trust in GOD and put this situation in his hands and continue to move on I had to feed them with a long handle spoon when I read in "Matthew 11:28:30 it says come to me, all you are weary and burden and I will give you rest, for your soul for my yoke is easy and my burden is light this scripture helped me get through this ordeal I was going through I could never imagine my daughters doing this to me everything I taught them about respect honor all of this had to happen to me I now look at my children in a different way now I love them. I don't trust them anymore it really sadden me and really hurt me from the bottom of my heart I just had to no matter what in letting the go I love them know I must love from a distance this story I told taught me a very good lesson I hear a lot of people say that it is your family will hurt you and destroy you if they can that was interested but what if it is your own children, I learn that you must "BE CAREFUL" it is very sad that I had to be careful of my own children I had to be careful of this snake this snake was lying outside frozen and there was a man walking into his home and looked down and seen this frozen snake the man bent over and picked up the snake took the snake into his home and the man preceded to help take care of the snake.

He laid the snake on the fireplace and the man kept on doing what he doing cleaning doing odds and in around the house he went in took a bath and came back out to see if the snake was still there the snake had crawl away the man started looking for the snake he looked everywhere could not find the snake finally the man turned around and the snake bit him the man ask the snake why you bit me I bought you in my home I nursed you back to health and the snake replied to the man" you knew I was a snake when you brought me into my home now the moral of my story is that I never thought that either of my daughter would actually turned against me now instead of letting other people into my home the whole time it was me daughters I had nursed them when they were babies until they were adults she then moved out and I let her come back into my home and the whole time she had a motive to try to destroy me and no matter how that hurt me she didn't care at all if I was out the picture now, I know now what to watch and look for I now can recognize a snake I thought it was outside people the whole time the snake was right in my face didn't have no clue that it was my own daughter lurking so now I am aware that a snake will put a grin or a nice smile on its face and pretend they care as for me daughter intentions were to hurt me and harm me she wanted to see how many times she could strike at me in "Roman 13: 8 it says Owes no one anything except to love each, for the one who loves another has full fill the law next story is about my second daughter as her growing up she was very quiet.

She never talked sometimes I never knew she was in the house she was very shy and so later in her teen years she started rebelling against me she started hanging out with the wrong friends and started becoming rude she was so disrespected, and she tried to be very controlling at 22-year-old daughter that had everything going good for her life had her apartment transportation in college had two adorable children I would come over to her home to see the grandbabies and the only way I could see them I had to report it was like I was being on a witness stand but the other grandmother could get them she would never ask no questions or anything I am them grandmother just like they were but I got treated just like I was not trust worthless to be around them so I told her I am leaving, and I will not be back she said OK that's fine with me that day was not over later I am at home sleeping and got a disturbing call on July 4,2015 my daughter was at home getting ready to go out and she had started drinking had the kids in the car and had her cousin in the car with her wanting to fix in with other people she let in the car drinking and driving got pulled over driving almost hundred miles per hour on the highway she was driving so fast she almost hit an elderly lady and she could had hurt herself and the kids and her cousin in the car it was a police officer on the side of the highway and pulled out and stopped her had her get out and walk a line she couldn't and told her to blow in the breathier and her blood level was very high well they took her to jail well they took the kids and cps took them and she had to do classes and other thing to get her children back she did everything she was to do to get her children back except having a home well that's when I came, she had to come back to me she asked me if she could come to stay with me until she gets a job and get a place and being the mother that I am I let Satan into my home I had to ask" GOD" to help me this was my day my life turn into a nightmare when I let her come in with the grandkids.

I just don't know why I did that me trying to help her and the grandkids it was not a day when she came in trying or calling herself trying to run my home telling me what I am to do in my home trying to tell me what I can or cannot do in I am I ask my cousin is someone is trying to play a prank on me or something I said I know this is not happening like this. I told her this is my home you remember that well as the weeks went on, she started telling her boyfriend he could come over and led into telling him he could spend the night I didn't know until my neighbor was telling me about it I worked nights and I addressed her, and she told me that this is her life, and I could not tell her nothing yes, I replied this is my home anyway it had gotten to appoint that when I leave and go to work she just let the kids just do anything in the house.

I ask her pick up behind her kids or wash up her dishes she says I do it when he gets ready it must be on her own time and I would ask me daughter why stir up trouble or call yourself to control your own life she will then tell me to shut up or put her earplugs in ignore me she walks around the house throwing bible verse or scriptures at me and turn around and slam the door in my face it would be days when I be taking care of me mom and daughter and she would just come in and take the remote control and put it on something we don't watch and tell us to deal with or if I am cleaning up the house and tending to my mom and daughter and I be so tired not asking do I need help she would sit and look it would be time and days that I just collapsed to the floor, and I would just be there until I come around to drag myself to get up and get into a chair she would sit there on the phone slander my name to her friends boyfriends or whoever she meets tell people that she wished I was not at my own home and I needed to get another place which she was living with me in her mind was to move in take over everything. I was told about this story when the middle daughter did this to me this story is about this blind girl who hated herself because she was blind. She hated everyone, except her loving boyfriend. Her boyfriend was always there for him.

She told her boyfriend one day "If I could just see the world, he told her boyfriend I would marry you'. So, one day the girl got the surprise that she always wanted someone had donated her a pair of eyes. When the girl bandages came off she could see everything including her boyfriend her boyfriend then asked her now my love now that you can see the world, will you marry me

His girlfriend looked at her boyfriend and seen that he was blind the sight of her boyfriend closed eye lids it had shocked the girlfriend the girlfriend hadn't expected that the thought of looking at her boyfriend for the rest of her life it gave her a changed mind that fast and the girlfriend refused to marry the boyfriend after he stood by her side the whole time she was blind. The boyfriend he got up tears in his eyes it wasn't a day later the boyfriend wrote his girlfriend a letter saying to her he told her take good care of my eyes my love before they were yours, they were mines. Now the moral of my story my daughter complained when I walked into the room the rolling of her eyes was ambivalent I felt I was displaced as the navigator in my life it had become her compass yet increasing I recognize that I will be I would ought to be displaced my daughter would make noise of exasperation and then her temper would instantly rise shooting up like a thermometer her temperature was always high. In fact, if I could stuff back those words back in her mouth I would lately I've become are of dissonance a dislocation as through a familiar text that had sudden become illegible to me as a mother it just seems like litany of force of insistence of exposition and declamation it seems suddenly to have contained too much of myself the status changes my daughter remember what life was like before.

And who was always by them side in the most painful was this is a very good lesson and an experience for me as I look at today world and society and see how much it has changed throughout the generation not just my children but the generations the kids are of control the emotional the needs love the sharing the bond I look at my children with the love unconditional.

All I wanted for them is not to suffer I have never did nothing to my children to make them treat me the way they have treated me or control or even hurt me or say hurtful thing to me the love I have for the I would never ever put them in any kind of harm way life to them was like fun flashy and fulfilling and having fun within themselves when it came down to me and my happiness it was like I was not to be at all I just sit and watch them be as I am a caregiver, twenty-four hour a day and running around and doing everything running around and doing.

Looking at my children it is unclear that they are when I conceived and being born it's the parent gratitude to me it the clad, and how I took care of them.it the obligation to me as a parent having with my children the neglectfully low to me I just wished my children would be more supportive and the understanding and not so abusive and disrespectful. the interesting thing my children had the nerve to ask me "why would you ask me" why would you write something like that." "Parents don't owe our children nothing well I don't it's the act of the expressive and the gratitude of owing. I would tell them that they owe it to themselves to build a good healthy life for themselves and to make right decision and making good choices when leaving out of parent home and not mess up their life and then want to fly back into to parent home life is not the problem it's the decision the child make life was unfaith that's what they would say to me looking at life it seems to hideously and unfair my children played a complicate for them to manage to learn all the pain they put me through and all the painful hurtful things they did to me the ubiquitous whether it's the disrespect the threats my children had felt obligation towards me loving them or loathe them is the vague sense the not fulfilling the indebted them to be unreflective and the ungrateful confusion that was rooted and the ambivalence about me I hurt all the time behind and the way they treat me.

The stories that that have been told are true for a mother to go through this they hurt me emotional I have done nothing to them for them to turn against me I could never or would never put my children through the pain they put me through I just don't know why they would want to control or would want me to do what they wanted to do as I continue to talk about the things, I have been through I talk about parents' emphases the responsibility of a child some would say that parents don't owe their children nothing I remember in a movie years ago a father grown son responded to his father that he owes his father nothing the child had that stated that he didn't ask for his father to bring into this world the father had tried to explain to the son that it was a reason why God wanted him to come into this world, but the boy was not trying to hear it.

I was always told a long time ago that behind a great man is his great mother my great role of a godly mother was my aunts' grandmothers and they have passed on to be with our lord what my children fail to realize is that we learn that sincere faith of mothers the combining instruction Timothy in the bible in his earliest day the scriptures the example results in Timothy life it shows that through faith in God by honoring his word godly mothers have great influence as they train their children.

Seeking help and understanding and support is one thing I just could not get I could support I know that to me was very hard as a parent who has grown children and how they have betrayed me in the manner of hurting me hypothetical given ultimatum were laced with bitterness I stated I'm still your parent but I guess you all don't really want to hear ever wise thoughts that crosses my brain and mind what happen and when for you suddenly found yourself in a broken eggshell world like sort of emerging you may need god's words more than ever the first verse that came into mind was pick your battle isn't that a verse stops your battles you can't control your own life without God Roman 12;18 as far it depends on me.

I will live at peace with all people Proverbs 20:11 even a child makes himself known by his acts by whether his conduct is pure and upright God world is so relevant in every situation and this is so true when discussing a rebellious child wise king Solomon wrote this verse describing how a child actions will define who he or she is or how he is accepted if a young person acts with purity and upright heart then he will be seen as joy and blessing.

However, if a child chose to disobedience and defiance then he will be labeled as rebellious and difficult there are many reason why a child might be oppositional and resistant to those in authority by the natural state of a man to sin so there is a propensity to rebellion in each one of us like KING SOLOMON EXPLAIN here we all fully bound up in our hearts now so must discipline to push you in the right way or the right direction Ecclesiastes 12:1 remember also your creator in the days of your youth before the evil days come and the years draw you near of which you say, I have no pleasure in them listen life can be hard as you face trials and challenges on daily basis it reminds as all that we need to focus on God and his will for us the earlier we turn our hearts over to him, the more problem and pit falls are lightly to avoid as stated at the end of the same chapter the end of the matter: all has been heard fear God and keep his commandments for this is the duty of man for God will bring every deed into judgement for ever secret thing whether good or evil Ecclesiastes 12:13:14 actions have consequences. The lord encourages us to choose wisely Mark 12:30 and you shall love the lord your God with your heart and all your soul and your mind with all your strength I believe this is a great verse because it shows exactly how we can combat defiant and disobedient heart there is no room left for insurrection to lift its heads in your lives focusing your attention on the lord, he will release you from your sin the lord is quick to forgive us for our sins when you repent and turn back to him so at the end of the day as a parent its more about relationship with our child and laying the law down I just didn't know what the problem I wonder why GOD left me on this earth with these hateful children, it just worried me.

I just wasn't sure about this situation I just didn't know how to approach my daughter I didn't know whether to get out of her way or just let her work for problem out I tried to talk to my daughter and let her know that life is too short not to obey your parent or even mistreat them you know it's more children are passing in this world now days as a mother you as my child should honor and respect me the person who gave birth to you it is not good in trying to tell your parent nothing because parents don't owe you nothing the more I try to talk the more she covers her ears or even walk out of my face or even say leave me along being the mother, I am as my heart get older and my soul was just crying out of pain she didn't care if my she had torn my heart this is deeper that it is I have always loved them my love will never change despite of all the things they have put me through the only thing I can do is to love them and hope the best for them and hope they would turn around for the best a wise person told me this story a long time ago as a parent you take care of your children and when there are eight to eighteen years old but as they get older, they engage in more risk behaviors it's like when they are four or five years old they play at the park or the playground on the swings or even running around soon as they reach twelve or fourteen years of age, they are interested in sports then as a parent we are afraid they will hurt themselves and then by the time they are sixteen they are driving getting their money on their own and around other people that they are around negative in their life but in reality it seems much actually they are simple able to their parents off and hide what's really going on once they hit that age of seventeen and twenty-two.

They have a lot of thinking errors it's like they have a spelling error or even misread a world or two life problems with the wrong solutions when life starts hitting them, they want to be the victim and want to put the blame on parents you may often hear them say I'm getting older now you should trust me but, their brain is still in there brain is in their twenties as a parent you can't succeed into thinking error consider your relationship well sustain to you as a parent there is a natural relationship between you in as much as they are the instruments of your existence the circumstance which seem to invest them the commonness of the tie takes off mind from contemplating its closeness its tenderness its sanity you is literally part of your if you love your parents, you will be delighted to be in there presents and

Your company will take the pleasure in being at your home you have to strive in always to please as a parent we are always anxious to please you as our children if whether we, please them or displease any person being obviously impossible t you can have all the affection towards the parents the essence of pity toward God is a deep solicitude to please him the essence of filial piety is solicitude to please your parent so be consider of your weight you put on your parent the obligation rest upon you for me to keep my head up and continue to move on as a parent I had to learn over and over the bible is the perfect medicine for this solution it was the perfect bible to turn in and read while I was going through my rough and tough times cast all your cares on the lord hand and lord will sustain you; he will never let the righteous be shaken Psalm 55:22 these are true promises with the seeds of inner hidden in them it not easy to misread the passage God is a problem solver casting our troubles means God will take our troubles away I just love this phase let go and let God because it sounds so simple but to me there were times when I wasn't clear what is it to let go and then there were times I just had to just let go sometimes there is and was a different in what I want to give up and what I wanted to release I was holding on to my children and all the time I thought that it was good for me.

But it wasn't. I even tried to show them not tell them for me to be free from all this trouble pain rejection the things that I had done for each one of my girls all the abuse and the abandonment verbally I was force to leave one place to go to another place to be happy it was very hard dealing with rude children all the bitterness and rudeness grudges had against me was very sad in this case when I told MY children to respect me and honor me as their parent it was like MY stomach had turned when MY children had treated me with such contempt it was like it was not for them to honor me as there parent IM so deeply hurt by them it was like the evil they had for me it was for them to seek retribution love for a hurting parent and a hurtful parent it does not come from the abilities its supernatural love of Jesus. In "Roman 5:8 you may feel that honoring your parents excuse your behavior. that is why they need to appreciate me while I have breath in my body cause when your mother is gone they are gone, cherish me while I'm here all the experiences that I had to go through to get myself stronger was to keep my faith in God the trials that I had was to teach my children to be strong teach them that's what I was trying to do be everyone else voice was more than mines the only thing I wanted to be to make a difference in their life I would tell them that life was not given to me I had to work for thing in life and it was not given to me freely, so it applied to them also life cannot be given to you freely.

I found myself with all the hurt and feeling and fear of issuing arising just simply just pushed everything under the rug now all the hurt that was pushed under the rug was coming out to make me understand and I had to accept it knowing in my heart that I was a good mother I did my best to the fullest to raise them as a single mother I am human also and I'm surely not perfect however I believe in my heart that I tried to protect them to my fullest I did everything a mother would do to help her children everything I did was from a place of love that was in my heart you know parenting do not have any instruction so I did what I thought would be the best to my abilities in raising them.

The poorly behavior they had they made those choices themselves you know as an adult you cannot forget your roots and the womb you came from and surely you cannot replace it with different family what can one say it is a very sad thing to say commentary indeed it is you and you will realize that no one take a place of a good parent no one can equal up to a good parent another parent will never have the same love as your own parent there way days in my life was so hard for me and there were days it was so dark there were times lots of stress mounted so high and unexpected diagnosis the devastating a difficult to face through I realize that my faith is mostly my strength and in my easy times of life but the most trying is often sometimes it was hard to walk out when you are swirling in the mist of everything that I had long the carefree it had gotten to a time where I had to fall to my knees and let God take my hand and lead me on and let me stand my body had gotten tired.

And I have gotten so weak God had to lead me through my dark times and had to keep going to my greatest strength character beauty and trust and my perseverance to the deepest part of my soul God as my desire my life ultimately to make me feel more like him to have the relationship God had to walk me through my dark times so I can come out on the other side Psalm 147:3 he heals the broken hearted and binds up the wounds. This is how it has been for the most painful experience in my life, and I have made it when your treasures in life are your children you have given all your strength your gifts services your energies time and anything you have done for them or did for them it became no part of their life anymore it just breaks your heart I know my children have always broken my heart in my mist of dealing with the difficult circumstances my when they broke my heart, I couldn't do nothing but cry all I could say is that they did the most to bring me down but did yell at them or reject them no I didn't know the thing I did or could say is nothing and return them Bach completely too our father in heaven I had to discover the God almighty cares about every detail of my life it has been shaken completely to the core God love is unfailing and his promises is always there to secure me so far, me journeys dealing with my children through the hopes healing and forgiving in Deuteronomy 31:8 he promises to be with us the lord is the one who goes ahead of you he will be with you. He will not fail you or forsake you.

Do not fear or be dismayed. The challenges that faced with confident that God is with me and God never lose sight of me, and the pain and God was still picking up the pieces God was always there loving and being understanding holding me and making a way out of nowhere there seem to me there was no way-out Psalm 34:19 God promised to deliver from despair the Lord is near to the brokenhearted and saves those who are crushed in the spirit many are the afflictions of the rightness.

But the lord delivered me out of them all struggling, hopeless I had to allow myself to be bogged down with regrets and the only thinking I had was if only I had hone this or even I had said thing different I just wondering where I went wrong the pain was like jumping into a bottom pit looking at them make bad choices and decision my life was turned upside down and the relationship was tested to the limit I served the loss of their innocence for their life as a mother I felt that everything had fallen apart right before my eyes I was heartbroken one of the most difficult things I had faced was the disobedient lying deceitful hurtful words they would say to me this made me so isolated I knew God understood my pain because God too is a father and his children have broken his heart repeatedly anytime you break God heart and causes him sorrow in Genesis 6:5:6 tells us that in the days of Norah on earth he is heartbroken in fact the lord was sorry that he made man on earth, and he was a grieved in his heart verse 6 my heart broken heart I faced seemed overwhelming and hopeless the circumstance was so different in terms but Christ was always there it was always hope the bible is full of Gods strength courage.

And I needed to make it through the difficult times victoriously of darkness and despair when the lord saw wickedness of a man as a great I had to do all these things for me to keep my head up and continue trust in my Godin had to shop very hard to keep my mind with God for me not to lose it so while my children continue to treat me, I just basically had to cut them out of my life they we're being very toxic to me and the thing I did was let them take advantage of me it would have been very good if they appreciate me appreciate me for who IAM I respect them, and I love them but until now and I will say until I come to my end of my journey that parents don't owe them children nothing IM not respond ability for their existence my children did not bring me into this world to be the child GOD brought me into this world to be a loving parent and all it all came from the bottom of my heart GOD expect the young to obey however the direction and the message that GOD have given us as parent s to give to our children, if you cannot obey your parents while you are on this earth how is you going to obey GOD," EPHESIAN" 6:1-3 "children, do what you parent tell you.

This is only right honor your parent tells you this is only right honor your father and mother is the first commandment that has a promise attached to it namely so you will live well and have a long life also in 1 JOHN 2:15-16 the message doesn't love world way don't love the worlds goods love the world of the world out love for the father practically everything that goes in the world wanting your own way wanting everything for yourself wanting to appear important has nothing to do with the father it just isolates you with all the discourages my children have put me through.

All though I had to endure all these situations with my children it was another thing I had to go through I have learned that when children move back home into their parent home it is an unpleasant tension and disagreement that has risen however adult children who moves back into their parent home they should avoid conflicts by following {1 first if they come back into parent home they should contribute what they should, and it don't always have to be in the term of money it should be time around the house {2 they should be productive family members that would help them earn them keeps. {3 be able to patriate in helping with mom dad grandmother grandfather etc..... with chores and errands or whatever needed to be done {4 when adults return home, they should respect them parent to rescue them from difficulties. {5 as adults' children the parent are not responsible for getting them out of their own scrapes or trying to avoid them in the first place {6 they must respect their parent lifestyle and their needs of independence what the parent is doing or has been doing since the children been gone, they shouldn't have to change anything they have been doing since the children had moved out of their parent home {7 the last thing is it is unrealistic to expect parents live to revolve around the needs of a grown child in the manner they may have when the child was younger. The chances that I gave my children the less respect they had for me or even given to me they are being ignore the standard that set me because they will not know no matter, they are already comfortable in disrespect I use to tell my children the way they treat me I use to tell them that when the devil keeps on asking you to look at your past there must be something good in it just like your future and that the devil doesn't want you to see even though they never tried to listen to me I also had to pray for them I had to get to myself, and these adult children pray this prayer for them Dear lord my children are no longer under my roof or under my wings are not out making them own life decisions of their own lord I give you back your children after praying that prayer a burden let up off my shoulder knowing that I had done all I could do for them it came to the crossroads that they were not thankful and that I could not believe it after they had gotten grown I didn't know how they could speak to me in this tone or manner or in such a way they had no gratitude I really didn't know they could be so no grateful to me.

I did my best as a single mother to provide the best for them all these years as a mother tired toward help but I was just spinning my wheels all it was just a game it was just a way for them to keep pushing my buttons the anger violence pressure it is very powerful it has really confused them the only thing we simply want for our children is to help them with the problem the more they have grown into maturity it seems like a touch the chances Psalm 139:10 trusting God will deliver us from despair the one who is able to heal and forgive and become whole again in Isaiah 26:3 he will keep in perfect peace all those who trust in him who thoughts turn in the lord when the storms of life came my way it was so hard but then it let the size of circumstances overwhelm me I asked how this happen what am I am going to do how will I make it through this the more I dwelled on the circumstances the deeper I had sunk I felt like I was drowning I had to change.

I have given over and over given them all the respect they still had less respect for me they just had none they have already made themselves comfortable in disrespectful I use to tell them that the way they treat me I would tell them that when Satan keep on asking you to look at your past there must be something good in it just like your future and that the Satan don't want you to see even though they never listen to me I just prayed for them I just had to get myself in a closet or room and drop to my knees and pray this prayer for them Dear Lord my children are still under my roof and under my wings and they are not making the right life decision of their own so lord I must place them back into your loving arms and shortly after that a burden came off my shoulders knowing that I had done everything I could do for them it was like everything had come to a crossroad.

And they just were not thankful at all I just couldn't believe it after they had gotten grown, they just didn't know how to speak to me in such a tone manner in a way they didn't have no gratitude had done the best for them as a mother all these years all I was doing was just spinning my wheels the violence pressure that was very powerful and confusing as a parent just your adults children look at you and proceed to do something at there were times that they wanted to control me the harder I tried to hold my ground the more brazen their effort to rock my sanity and undermine my sanity and undermine my authority of being a single mother there were several well-trod and unpleasant paths.

I felt so unappreciated everything they were doing to me the perception that my children was so unpleasant to me why they felt the need to mistreat me I really don't know the feeling I had was like in the inside of me was like a you know when you're in bed at night and you hear a faucet dripping and nearly if you are reasonable rested you would fix it the leak before it happens you must find the right tools to fix the leak the leak now you go to sleep set aside a questor hour the next day you get the tools to replace the washer the end of the story the leak doesn't rock your emotional boat now if you are short on rest your moment needs are throbbing that sounds can kick up feeling or upset it can trigger feeling of the last straw when you don't know how to fix a leak and you don't have the tools to fix the leak then you have the moment to yourself for the past two or three monumental the faucet is to blame that does them pretty much defend for themselves.

So as a parent I had just had to move out of the way and let them fall and let them call back on God to pick them back up letting God step in to teach them a lesson is what I had to do I know adult kids get frustration they have to realize that they cannot get their parents exhausted especially when they have moved back into their parents' home in many situations the feeling of resentments the adults' children seems to feel that they are entitled to meals money gas money when they do nothing but sleep and party all night or they think they can take their anger frustration out on their parents or if we ask them to pitch around the house or even give you're a thank you for being who we are now they think because they are adults and living in their parents' home its fine to be lazy no!!!!

They are just trying a quick way out over the time when children become adults the stop learning how to solve problems and entrain themselves because they are adults, they are quick to find a way out this takes me back to this TV show into our generation in the 1970s and through 2000s.

I don't know if a lot of you remember this TV show the little house on the parries it was a life of a family and a young girl named Laura now laurel has encountered who grew up as a frontier each week Laura encountered new situation opportunism to come about her life and the developments values morals and taking responsive and conflicts she had with Nellie now Nellie was the local bully now as the story goes on nelly falls in love with a boy that did not love her back her family struggled with that with a piece of chalk and a new pair of shoes and celebrated ok now as the story goes on Laura respects her parents and the most important thing each family had a purpose thing to do and as a role in the family laurel helped her mother to care for her sibling her oldest sister did the sewing to contribute meaning that everyone pitched in and helped as a family to help the family it allowed her to experience the struggles as she learned she could overcome the adversities her mother did not run to Nellie mother every time there was an argument.

They found was to work it out it was a message Laura received the message I have is as parents we don't owe you children nothing it is so sad to see this adult young generation must run back to their parents when they have a problem when you enter adulthood mom and dad isn't their always to fix thing they don't know what to do as when you become an adult and you get into trouble and then you run back home for them to solve your problem for you then has many remain in their parents' home sitting on their parents couch sleeping in their beds rather than moving out these days they have no clue what gens they have in their parents who as another story to tell I use to tell my children this all totally care for them and who is raising them.

When I raised my children ages from 1 year to eighteen and then they let the nest came back in twenty they turned on me except for one that I'm raising, and she is disable to me how can you be an adult if you don't try to learn the basic of growing up in your parents' home is where you start you have your teaching and you're learning, and you grow into maturity and become your own person as an adult as you are at home us as parents teach you to grow to become adults not hurt you nor bring you down but make sure you can live in this world in 2 Timothy 3:1 understand this that the last days there will come times of difficult people will be money lovers abusive disobedient to their parent ungrateful unholy heartless unappeasable slanderous without self-control brutal not loving good treacherous we are living in the last days also, in if you look in Ephesian 6: children obey your parents for it is right I will start with us children for an example if you are twenty-two years old and still play with your x box, PlayStation for nine hours a day and still live with your parents you need to get out and get a job and move out and honor your parents but you will tell yourself you don't have to live them well.

Why did you come back home then get your own place and to say you don't have to live with the rules in other ways you are thinking your parents are still paying the bills if you are an adult, you must look at the big picture well that makes you still a child because you are too lazy to get out to get a job or even be on your own or even want to pay your own bills or get your own place so their fourth you must obey your parents though you are still in their home no matter if you are an adult the rules still apply because you came back to them.

They didn't ask you to come back when you left the first time when you turned eighteen the rules were there and when you decided to come back the rules stilled applied the rules never went away but you have the nerve to come back into your parents' home expecting things to change or thinking they owe you something why no they don't. listen all of you young adults that call you self-adult and still at home that are probably saying um you just don't know my parents are ridiculous think about this in the end about if other creatures in the creator realm rebelled like children speaking just what if you cross an antelope of the plain of Africa just going forget your mom to the lion so he runs at the lion and starts targeting the lion rather than listening to what the mom is saying got to do this there like no in the world there are thousands and thousands of lions killing us you may think you are getting away the first time or even the second time.

Eventually he will eat you I'm going to say these parents are not responsible for your actions and your existence if you do not bring us parents into this world, we brought you into this world God brought us parents in this world to be the loving parents we are and everything we do as parents comes from the bottom or heart even when we must chastise you that's from God this message God have given us as parent to our children if you cannot obey your parents while we are on this earth how is you going to obey God this is only right how can we as parents hand off our faith to you one of the main trainings in gods words a mother must grow in her own her own love for gods words I know from experience so when we point and guide you in the right direction it is a point of target in our eyes it shouldn't have been dismissed it is a fair hearing and an evaluated in the light of God word and prayer.

It's the supreme love for a parent to have love for their child as a parent the dissipate the clouds of darkness that have causes peace to our heart when a parent have stuck by you ageless 1 john 2, 15:16 says the message don't love words way don't love the worlds good love the world of the world out of love for the father practically everything that goes in the world wanting your own way wanting everything for self-wanting to appear important has nothing to do with the father it just isolates you with all discourage although we as parents had to endure all these situations with you children's it another thing to go through we as a parent we must learn that when adults move back into the home it can or could be unpleasant for us there could be a lot of tension disagreement that will take a rise when the move back into the home now I believe that if you move back in the home I think you should contribute of what you can, and it don't even always have to be terms of money it can be your time around the house you should be productive, and you be able to pastorate in helping your parents around the home with chores and errands or whatever need to be done and the last thing it is unrealistic to expect parents to live to revolve the needs around the home as all the contemptuously towards me the precepts have force their ripe age love cannot exemplified when you were in the wound and ever step gentle and I was careful not to bother you while you were sleeping in the womb when you began to enter the world I turned and started on forcing on you as you enter the world now as a parent what exactly do, we owe you were giving the best thing from your parents and that was life we owe you nothing but to treat us and respect us as parents the obligation that are legally enforced mostly the right-thinking adult children are lightly as adults in two ways you have the right as a positive provision that may not enjoy that parent has the duty that pessimistically in the development full rationally in the bible prophecy disobedience to a parent unthankful unloving forgiveness slander adult children get stuck when becoming as adults when they move back into their parents' home and try to mess their life up once you let that child move back into the home they think after they come in.

We are obligated to give them all our time and attention to them then they start wanting to play their aces card so now they play the victim role Really, they want to make us parents feel guilty and say I can't move along that puts a strange on the parents you as adults' children must realize that as a parent, we have a right to be in peace and not punching bag parents have a right too we shouldn't have to give up our life to come to your rescue or help it's a line when your grown you must take care of your own problems we are parents to stand behind you for support when a parent state their issue and problem ore we are upset that you as adults' children wants to live in the home and take other people sides without a balance when a parent has been hurt badly when they can't move along or they can't afford to be on their own that is the most powerful tool or thing phrase move along as an adult you would say to you to make them feel or say or guilty or even pity for them I just want in plain English language that's a discomfort shame let me as this question how do you as adults take the respond ability for your financial help from your parent or react to it know I'm going to split hairs, you cannot afford your lifestyle because it is prudent to find both cause financial short falls as well as a solution how can you cover basic expense creating financial solution out in the air well there it goes again both problem your problem is not your parents it's not even society or the government problem the problem is yours the longer its yours the longer it will remain it's still going to be your problem parents have already done what they had to do in raising you they still made ends meet and provided the basic thing you needed it's good to be compassion at times to help you out at some point I'm not going to be completely self-centered the problem that I have is the emotional blackmail you in order to make you feel way and the pressure they feel from the parent you adults play upon guilt for a parent to feel sorry for you and give to you so there forth parents don't like to be pressured and no parent like to be pushed into a situation out of obligation that's why I say we don't owe you nothing in proverbs, "8:23-33 Now therefore listen to me, my children for blessed are those who keep my ways hear instruction be wise, do not disdain it when you have disrespectful children that leave home and come back when already piece in your home and the comeback in thinking they can come back in thinking they can take over that's not good or right I have learned, and I notice that adult children have lots of challenging in today society.

My children are concerned about what they are entitle to or what they deserve all the griping and the complaining of what they didn't get or what they are supposed to get or even what they deserve or even what they should get I look at life and now at all the demands me as a parent don't feel guilty as a parent as I am, and I know there are things we do as a owe our children and then there are thing in life that we do not owe thing and as a parent I have proved that our unconditional love and our respect forgiveness they deserve a place to call home food to keep them healthy a good education that will help them alone the way what else do we owe our children as I stated nothing cause as a parent we have given all we can give them we will still love them and guide them all the communication praying for them all that we give them as babies totters teen until reaches adulthood.

I will still pray for them they should keep or consideration. That just like in PASALM 119:9 How can a young person stay pure by obeying your word and following its rules. It is a fearful thing to see and hear how my children takes contemptuously towards me all the precepts to my children have force them of their ripe age if I only had the natural incapacity which they bear down to the weak degree I was always taught children are supposed to honor their parents and their speeches the lifestyle my children when they got grown, we as parent don't owe them that lifestyle anymore my question is what do we owe "Nothing" the obligation that are legally enforced

Mostly the right to think that my children would be unlikely to treat me this way still to this day I don't know.as a parent my duty was enforced to provide for their welfare and to enjoy the right and the indeed obligation to treat paternalistically in their development full rationally my duty as a parent is the right like ought to imply or even may it to prevent my children from harm "Jesus called out the Pharisees and scribes for your disobeying God our instruction comes from God.

So if we don't respect us then your disobeying Gods commandment in "Proverbs" 23-22 it says Harken unto your father that begat thee and despise not your mother and your mother and your father when she gets old the tenor of the scriptures indicates respect of parent while they are young and before they become elderly you really must read "proverbs" especially without getting a picking up an attitude.

Looking at my children and the days they don't have the ability to consent to waving their rights the thinking in their heads to think that parents owe them something you know it is really time that for all you adults quit saying that we owe you something, but I never heard you say how do we get to OUR FATHER'S HOME a lot seems to be headed in the wrong direction on this earth it is like a navigation system and like the today's smart phones children uses their phones to navigation to lead us in the direction here and there but as the world goes on the world revolves around technology no one never ask the pastors or the mothers of the church its always what we owe them but how many adults' children ask that question how to get to OUR FATHER HOME that's something you never hear your adult ask they never say what path do we need to take to get to OUR FATHER HOME its easy and very simple you just must pay attention first you are headed down Sin ALLEY you will find a dead-end road that ends in DESTRUCTION avoid that road quickly and make a U TURN and head towards REPENTANCE ROAD make a right watch out for the POTHOLES detour that is going to lead you to INDEPENDENCE this sign will lead you wrong you will go until you reach a sign of REPENTANCE stay on that road until you get to the sign that read BELIVERS keep straight until you come to a green light which is called JESUS CHRIST.

You have now reached GRACE ROAD this lane turns into FORGIVENESS stay on this street until you get to a curve it's going to turn into BRIDGE OF FAITH then you are going to run into some TROUBLED WATER keep going that is going to lead you to PRAYER PARKWAY and there you will be find for one day take that place and this place will be a WORD OF WISDOM that's the life place for all your scriptures you will also find your answers to all your question that you may have in life and the HELPER STREET is a good place for your GUIDANCE to your truth as you continue your way the next street you will run into you will have to YEILD and don't go to TEMPTATION STREET please whatever you do please avoid that wrong turn for your sake pass up EVNY, GRUDGE, HATE, LYING, and pass up GOSSIPING whatever you do pass it up those are the streets to stay away from that BLVD also pass up and avoid PITY DOUBT PRIDE bypass these roads for your own sake please DETOURE all these lanes they are not good for you because it will take you back to the beginning of SIN ALLEY for DEPRESSION as you continue you must take a right it runs completely into VICTORY Street just keep your head up until you come to a long white sign that

says YOU HAVE REACHED YOU DESTINATION TO THE KINGS HIGHWAY TO YOUR HOME THIS IS WHERE GODHAVE A SPECIAL PLACE PREPARED FOR YOU YOUR ETERNITY "Ephesian 5:31 to step out in his own as an adult comes his own conviction and rules the thing adult kids owe them parent even after them out of their parent home and out from under their direct authority honor the fifth commandment we all apply to small children growing up it also apply to adult children.

Also, even when still in their home you are still under their direct authority there home you still have to honor them. As a parent the discover the lines that become increasing you know there are a lot of children in the world begging and wanting a good mother and father and there are some that has lost their mother and fathers there are lots of parents are in jail prison and drugs in nursing homes in mental home hospital or even dead and there are those that just don't want to have nothing to do with them and that's very sad and then you have children that have the best or great parent and they are so disrespected ungrateful that goes back to "Matthew" 18 "Jesus told this story of a slave who owed his king a great deal of money the slave begged for more times his debt later the slave confronted a friend who owed him a little money the friend begged for more times but the king thrown him in prison when the king discovered what happened he had the slave tortured until he repaid all that he owed ", my heavenly father will also the same to you if each of you when you get grown all the demands you think you are entitled to the tone in our voice you hear how we speak with authority as you are older you may hear different tones in the TV radio news and other broadcast my question is it society setting you for your future is that your future is that what you are entitled to is to get everything you want. Sometime when I'm walking into the stores now I would often here children four to five or maybe even ten to fifteen years old say you promise to get me this or get me that and try to make the parent feel guilty that's the same when you get grown try to make us feel guilty now there are many things in life that we do owe you we owe you our unconditional love, respect as you should do the same for us respect us as parents our boundaries and we do the same as your boundaries we owe endless and the forgiveness food to keep your healthy education that would help you in life it so bothers me so dearly much that now and days you play sacrifice merely to have disagree with them as adults do you want to do what you are supposed to do in your parents' home they will state to the parents that we are parents and say we are ungrateful and I'm not talking about the small children.

I'm talking about the twenties and up who are capable of how and what they should control their parent lives with their parents you still have the need to make their decision knowing that it would hurt us we don't owe you our every minute every hour of the day every minute that goes around the clock now when you were babies, yes, you needed us because you couldn't do for yourself now you have to accept the decision and the condition your parents have brought you this world have so many deprivations and as many adults you must get adjusted to many thing desires will be left unsatisfied dreams will be crushed many hopes will be crushed, and some dreams will be destroyed you that this is so true we as parents prepared our off springs for the real world we are your guides of your youth and your counselors as parents we are your parents of teachers your consultant the response of which to be received with pious respect even though you have suspected the solidity and astuteness of your judgement it is due to vellum in within laying the matter before them and obtaining their opinion.

You as adults has the right to confine in their wisdom you

are still inexperience the path of life is considered to a degree that is untrodden to you the perplexities and perpetually arising which you have yet acquired no experience to understand you stand to them for your understanding nothing with all I'm staying just be happy of what you have and what you got and learn to listen and adjust to the world and thing your parents are trying to prepare for you and your life and just remember that your parents don't owe you nothing in your life there comes a threshold into adulthood once that line is cross the parent relation is supposed to change in so many basic ways in the precise line of demarcation it plays an important journey in 1 Corinthian 13:11 when I was a child, I talked liked a child though like a child I reasoned like a child when I became a man, I put my ways of childhood behind me as a child you have been done grated into a position of self-responsibility in which you are accountable to a higher authority the authority of God himself in God eyes under jurisdiction that a child transition to a self-determining entitle does this mean that children have prerogative to a dismissing attitude toward you or to disparage your values as a parent in Philippians 2:3:4 nothing out of selfish ambition or vein conceit rather in humility value others above yourselves not looking to your own interests but each of you interests of others as parents we teach you to live no matter what we teach you how to bloom and where you are you are planted; we have taught you to help others you must remember who you are and who God is God would not want you to think that us as parents owe you as parent, we love you and just want the best loving and honoring your parent does not equal obeying God has placed you with your parents for a reason and a season of a time to help you grow into mature into an adult at some point these seasons will end at some point of the relationship with your parent to adulthood it will change from child to parent from adult to adult the rules will change from dependency and authority to mutuality therefore you must respect your parent and stop thinking we owe you must respect and care for us as parent you are no longer under their tutelage and their protection we have told you how to travel the road and know it's turning its dangers and its difficulties whenever you runout of places to go and treat your parents like crap knowing that you would have to come back to them with your concerns and consult them on different subject companion and the book of recreation let parents be the receptacle of your ear and the receptacle of your cares you know into day world youth and as adult children you have lost so much respect for your parents who had worked so hard in raising you to be who you are it's like these days you have made derogatory remarks and pretend you cannot hear what parents are saying now adults listen in the end you will learn that you are your own person children you think that just because your parents are still on this earth and in your present we still owe you something you will get treated in life of how you treat your parent the idea of respecting your parent make no sense than the reverse which is respecting respect is earned and being older you take

it to your heart unless you recognize and confirm your life and focus on

having your own life and taking charge and quite expecting your parents

owe you your life would be better you cannot give nothing away you

don't have as you change yourself you will remember what your parent

taught you the love and understanding caring and being compassion

towards others not hurting them or feeling you want to be truthful

tell the truth and you will learn to give the affection to your parents

I just want to take a minute and I just you to see just take and look at

reality and see how this reflect on you look at this who was there when

you started walking, talking nursed you we sat up with you and when

had to go to work and you wanted to sit up and play even though you

wanted to play we stayed up with you made sure you didn't go hungry

you had a full stomach and learning how to speak, your first words who

kept a roof over your head learned you how to drive made sure you got

the education you needed and then you consciously choose to ignore

us as parents even though some parents are single as myself our love

is a very unconditional no matter what we made sure you were ok so

why all suddenly act like as if we as your parents owe you something

as a parent are doing you a favor by just standing in our existence you

should treat you're a queen for all the favors that we have done for

you and never asked you to repay us we only ask respect and to love

us as parents unfortunately the truth utterer disrespecting than it has ever been the endless worries and the care for you as children when parents have a choice it's based on parents don't owe their children nothing it is a conflicting opinion and reasonable expectations like I said before the obligation is owing is not the point don't get me wrong I love my children I hate the way they treated me it's like they have something against me I have tried to be the mother they wanted me to be compassion loving understanding mother for them but they have a certain experience or certain experience for me to learn certain things that I experience was the best thing that I could ever go through and experience I know I had to go through thing in order to understand and I know one thing that occurred the loss of traditional influenced can be hard for some parents and when they still domineer adult children who still consent to submit to their dominance parent authorities it takes a bold act of independence to break dependency then the adult child stubborn embraces a new life path that adopts new lifestyle's or life partner's that parent disapproved and so when the question criticizes the oppose the decision they want to stand with defiant of independent this is my life the recall I will live it as I please but to say why move back in your parents' home if it's your life there are question I've been thinking why you as adults say what I owe my parents who knows you know something you might think that you owe a lot then other times you may think why I should do something for them I have my own life so you could say in the day world children simple forget about their parent existence to them they may believe that no one asked their parents to have them it was our choice to be responsible and raise the next generation so if you look at the picture nature would find creatures who do something to support their parent after they are grown up we are just one of the creatures on earth with feeling lots of knowledge procreating their land so adult children you must look after the people that are close to you and then look at others or even look after others why do you forget sometimes your parent know this is the one reason of the thing that occurred to me in the mist I have touched a topic that seems to be especially important to me right now during my turbulence times in psalm 46:1:3 God is our refuge and the strength and ever-present help in trouble therefore we will not fear, through the earth and give away the mountain fall into the heart of the sea through its waters power through faith in Christ I was given a spirit of power love and discipline and the reason I had to go through even though me darkest days in 2 timothy 1:7 for God did not give us a spirit of timidity but a spirit of power of love and self-discipline all my hard time came, and God was there with me God was there with me through it all although I was not promised an easy life, I knew that, and I knew Christ was there I believed in Christ.

And I knew that he would not give me no more than I can handle because there were days I thought I wouldn't make it in 2 Corinthian 2:9 my grace is sufficient for you and me power is made perfect in weakness and in peter 5:10 and the God of all grace who called you to his eternal glory in Christ after you have suffered a little while. For aim the lord your God the holy one God gave me the spirit Exodus 33:14 my presence will go with you I will give you rest I didn't wonder if I would have trials, I expected them, but the good news is I don't have to face those trials alone God of the universe was watching when my children put me through what they put me through in the disobeying talking back cursing me out I was able to call on GOD and he encourage me to go through his word in Jeremiah 32:27 behold I am the lord the God of all flesh; is anything too difficult for me I often though that my trials were too big for me well it's not too big for the almighty God can handle everything that I went through when my trials seem like it would never end God is a God of all times he knows exactly how long our trials will endure and he gave me strength I needed to get through.

In Deuteronomy 31:6 be strong and courageous do not be afraid or tremble at them for the lord your God is the one who goes with you he will not fail you nor forsake you when I was facing all these trials with my children, I didn't know what Godhead planned for my future I had to just let him take my hand and guide me in the right direction he knows best for us his infinitely know more about me and my life more than I did God was just sitting and he was waiting for me for me to bring my problem and give them to him I really thought I could help or work the problem out but it was too much for me to handle so there forth

I had to give everything to God and let the almighty work it out in his favor instead of me leaning to my own understanding God understood he was able to handle what I was going through and what I was facing God was under my doubt when his thought my doubts as they creep in in the bible even Thomas and Peter had doubts still God encourage me that he will sustain me for no matter how shaky things were for me through everything God was and is he is my rescuer God was the one who came when I called out to him God was there.

He brought me out brought me back to safety when I though nothing was going right in my life I can acknowledge that I know God gave me all the protection and his angles surrounded me when I called out to God, he responded God didn't watch me when I was in trouble, he delivers me out and he honored and blessed me with a long-life God showed me that he was looking out for me all I had to do was to call on him through the precepts to the children not so much force to them to riper age because their natural incapacity and there childish passion and the passion and pleasure which bear down their weak degree of reason yet some what the measure of reason which is exercised to be delighted to be in their company be liked those unnatural children that love company and the idle play fellow better than their parents remember that you have your being from them and come out of their lions remember what sorrows you have cost them and how we care for you teach you must bloom and where you are you are planted we have taught you to help others we have taught you to help others you have to remember who you are and who is God wouldn't want you to think that us as parents owe you as a parent.

We love you and we just want the best loving and horning your parents does not equal obeying God has placed you with your parents for a reason and for a season of a relationship with your parent to adulthood it will change from child to parent and from adult to adult the rules will change from dependency and authority to mutuality therefore you must respect your parent
because we do care you are no longer under their tutelage and their protection, we have told you
how to travel that road and know it's turning its danger and its difficulties?

Whenever you run out of places to go and treat your parents like crap knowing that you will have to come back to your parents with your concern and consult them on the subject companion and the book of recreation let that parent be the receptacle of your ear and the receptacle of your cares you know into day world youth and raising you to be who you are its like you children these days have moth derogatory remarks and you pretend you cannot hear what your parents are saying now child's that are adults listen in the end you will learn that you are your own person children you think that just because your parents are still here on earth and in your present, we still owe you something you will get treated in life of which is respecting respect is earned and being older take this to your heart unless you recognize and confirm your life and focus on having your own life and taking charge and quit expecting your parent owe your life would be better you cannot give nothing away you don't have as you change yourself.   You   will remember what your parents taught you the love and understanding caring and being compassion towards others not hurting them or their feeling you must have affection towards your parent and you will see that you will have more confidence if you want to be truthful tell the truth and you will learn to give the affection to your parent like I was saying before the obligation is owing is not the point don't get me wrong, I didn't like how me children treated me and I love them dearly the loss of tradition influence can be hard when they still domineer and still consent to submit to their dominance parent authorities it takes a bold act of independence to break dependency then the adult stubborn embraces a new path that adopts new lifestyles when parents disapprove questions criticize the oppose decision they want to stand with defiant of independent this is my life as I recalled I will live it as I please the provision you must remember the tenderly we have loved you unconditionally and what grief it has been tour hearts for all of you and all we have done for you we as parents take happiness or misery of our own life you as young adults deprive us as parents of our happiness, and you deprive yourself of your own life when you reach adulthood and through you the chide you and the restrain to correct you as adult abate your love for us listen be content with your parent provision for you and the disposal of you do not rebellious against your parents and complain of your usage of their home as much lesson take anything against their will that is fleshly that is part of fleshly rebel and not be disobedient it is part of fleshly it is to be discontent because the fare not better because of the better clothes and because they have money to not allow you to spend or use at your own discretion let me ask you a question is you not under the government.

And I'm not talking about the world government I'm talking about the government of your parent and not your enemies are you lust and pleasures govern than your parent discretion you must be thankful of what you have remember that you deserve it not as you are freely it's your pride and your sensually it's your sensuality and it is not wisdom or vital that is in you must get your fleshly minds and not be so eager another question what if your parents did hardly to you in the food and raiment or expense what harm will do to you would have selfish mind sensation mind you would make a great deal it is very dangerous to your mind and body to be a bred to high and feed too much and daintily to bread to low and fed too hardly if you are a bible reader and read the bible it talks about how the earth open and swallowed all those rebellious murmurers that grudged against Moses and Arron pay attention adult children in this book of numbers 16.

It will apply to you and if you remember the story of rebellious Absalom and the folly prodigal Luke 15 and the desires to be your own disposal you have your own disposal you have the egger vein desire and have the heart fulfilled as an adult you have to contentedly submit to your parents in God way and expect your blessing but when you carvers yourself you may expect the punishment of rebels so why dissect every moment why assume that you are trapped in fate that dictated by your life choices you hold on to grudges throughout your whole life as a parent we did what we could do just because you see things differently it is not done not to imply that the prevision ways of thinking is wrong you know people through the world was flat and we all know the world is round and at one point in the time parents didn't have the technology or capabilities to know the true shape of the earth it does not mean parents were wrong thinking stupid or incompetent parents' decision is based on what they know, and you can't blame us for that you adult children you are like that you must figure out the earth is round where us parents thought it was flat, we are not dumb or dumbfounded but we are proud of your discoveries so stop patronize us because on day and you can rest for sure you will see how hard it is to raise a person even if you are not a parent at some point in time in life you will realize that we are parents and we are humans susceptible to making mistakes just like you as parents we are good living when we are going on with the lord, we are gone no need to cry and say if I could have should have done things different would, could, should have don't done different no it already done listen children we are parents for a reason we are Gods words if we are parents of God words and serve those who fear him let him be an example to you let the love that us as parents must engage you imitation a wicked child of godly parents is the one of the miserable children how can this be as a parent look at her child like that when parents are eminent for godliness and daily instruction salvation pray for you and warn you about destruction and you neglect the way your parents it is a shame you will never know how to build your house until you have tested all the elements and the heavy rains reveal the quality of the roof the high winds and the cord is how you are determining how your house will look the insulation the heat and the sun will determining the quality of the painting of siding therefor when you have all the quality then you have a solid foundation now it's ready to be laid to make your home secure and a good lasting stab able place to live now the moral of this is a lot of you adult children fine that we have given lip service to Gods command you are faced with reality and the foundation are not as strong enough for Gods weathers in life storms but then you must ask and question yourself how you react when your trials hit you do you worry or do you take like in your own hands how do you respond inappropriately when you don't get what you want or see God uses time to help us to recognize our foundation is sand or rocks you must ask God, lord if you built on this rock if so, could you be comfortable to know whether you prepared for the storms to come your way when your light has blinded you that would be dreadful judgement all tears teaching and the good example of their parents and their parents will witness against them.

And how they will be confounded before the lord and how sad through the hearts of parents their pain must witness against the graceless children as parents we taught you better and walk the exemplary life in today's world as a parent I had to focusing on God and the ability to bring you safety and through John 14:27 peace I will leave you with peace I will give you not as the world give do I give to you do not let your heart be troubled

This takes me back to a season of life where this woman that had four daughters this woman wanted her daughters to learn not to judge things so quickly so this mother sent each one of them on a quest for a test so each one of them she sent on this quest each one of these daughters had to look at a pear tree that was great distance away ok the first daughter had her mission to complete her mission in the winter the second daughter had to complete her mission in in the spring and the third daughter had to complete her mission summer and the last daughter had to complete her mission in the fall now all had gone and come back they called their mother and then these girls started each one of them began to describe what they had seen the first daughter said mother that tree I seen that tree was very ugly and twisted the second daughter said no mother it was covered with green buds and full of promise now the third daughter said I disagree mother it was laden with blossoms that smelled so very sweet and it was so beautiful it was most graceful thing I had ever seen the last child said my mother I disagree with all my sibling she said it was ripe and drooping with fruit full of life and fulfilment so, the mother explains to all her daughters that they all were right because they each seen the season in the trees of life now the moral of the story is that you cannot judge a person by only one season and that the essence of those who they are and to and the joy and pleasure love that come from that life you can only measure at the end when all the seasons are up now if you give up when its winter you will miss the promise of your spring the beauty of your summer fulfilment of your fall please pay attention don't judge a life by one difficult season don't let pain of one season destroy the rest of all the rest. now adults you can say you owe your parents instead of us owing you know us as parents are not perfect, but you can't be grateful if your parents have stuck with you.

And by you and stayed by your side and being there for you and kept on loving you it can be hard for your parents or any parent that would love you rambunctious from you being one year old and we loved you then and loved you through your teen rebellious years and love you until your adult years and your age all that time you nearly drove them crazy, they are parents and you should treasure if your parents have stuck with you growing up and you have reached adulthood that parents care, and that parent loves you that parent cares about you no matter what and if we cared then we care now on top of all some of you adult children have even more important reason to be grateful for your parents you have been blessed with parents who been more to you beside feeding hugging you helping you parents have showed the truth of God we have introduced you to Jesus, parents have great stories of the bible and as taught you Gods commands your parents have living in faith in Jesus and they have done things to help you learn to pray and the one thing is to help you know God that is a great privilege the obvious way is to reject your parents and everything they represent you reject them and reject their faith you have reject their way in life and you as children are proud of that and proud of yourself for doing so as you see it they follow what God has instructed them to do and you don't like your parents because of the rules they have for their home "Really" and that make you feel some type of way or make you feel superior to them the bible in Proverbs 30 verse 11:13 there are those who curse their fathers and do not bless their mothers those who are pure in their own eyes are yet not cleansed of their filth. those who eyes are ever so haughty those who glances so disdainful so when you look at you parent with disdain it's a natural look of their God with disdain you want nothing to do with your parent another way to turn away from your parents' faith in Jesus is what I call the "THANKS; BUT NO THANKS approaching.

Perhaps you appreciate your parents very much your ungrateful for all they mean to you ungrateful for all they mean to you, but don't you want to be kind to them in their home you enjoy moving back in there home you enjoy siting down on Sunday dinner but you're not eager to respect them but you think they are old fashion but the decision your choices and how you chose was a different way of your life for you in meanwhile you would settle into an unspoken agreement with them, you mock us as parents and then you turn around to say we nags you, but you are in our home looking for hand out and say that we owe you when you start turning against us as parents when you start seeing us to living for the lord you adult children you fear us, and we become a threat to you, so you pretend to be something you are not you want to say we owe you something you must be thankful for your parents now if you have been blessed with good parents that are pursued by God meaning by eternal canyon that no one can ever cross the canyon between heaven and hell that moment have not arrived yet Godin his grace continue to call you, you may shut your ears to us as parents, you may even ignore, us and you may even tell us to shut up and leave you alone or tell us not to talk to you, but does that stop God, he rebuts you and avoiding him and continue to call you, listen to what God says in the bible speaking about loving parents.

So I urge you to listen to your parents you have been hurting your parents in thinking they owe you something let my say to those of you who were blessed with good Christian parents who had stood by your side and provided for you so what I have been saying the whole time is to be grateful for your parents just think how delighted we would be as parents when `you give us your support and honor us instead of thinking that we owe you something we don't owe you we have been giving you everything we have giving you your life what do you do when your child goes way ward and how do you pursue how they have hurt you

These are question to me that are fraught with my pain and confusion as a mother the pain and confusion that stepped into my life with my children thinking I owe them something in its paradoxical that is true all of this goes back to Adam and eve you know sometimes purses by releasing us and if you can see this biblical insight with humanity falls which falls into Genesis 3 the fall the serpent was craftier than any wild animals the Lord God had made.

He said to woman, Did God really say, you must not eat from any tree in the garden" now you have to take a closer look God could have put angelic guards around this tree of the forbidden of fruit to play interference but he didn't God didn't want contrived and coerced obedience instead, he let us ancestors freely exercise their love for him and his word through obedience or consequences a necessary corollary when us as parents rejects the goodness and the beauty and faithfully fulfilling their God ordained roles, their father released them to the consequences, God consequences for Adam and eve included a dose of reality a taste of what life without God is like the taste would serve the redemptive purpose of awaking them in their need for God`s grace as their own hope God did not leave them in Eden, but he did let them go there and experience it's the result in which led to redemption this also go to the Prodigal son we all know this story as well son prematurely ask his father for his inheritance; the father obliges, releasing his inheritance; and releasing his son; son leaves, and squanders said inheritance, only to return home to his father after hitting rock bottom; father receives son back with open arms, only to alienate his responsible son.

Jesus' parable is so memorable because it's a universe who hasn't known so called prodigal this father release his son one of the most loving thing he could do when we release prodigal to the fruit of their choices instead enabling them Gods redemptive work has a chance to run its course were no longer in charge of the outcome we relinquish any influences we must give that person and the situation to God as I reflect on my own as a parent of adult children, I realize that parenting adult is about loving and accepting while I let go of all the worries and pain I really needed to and letting go of giving the advice to them they were not listening to me any way it's all about accepting choices and decision clearly, they won't always be the same this little girl and this apple tree there was a huge apple tree and there was a girl who always loved to play around the tree everyday this little girl would play around this apple tree she would up to the top of the tree so one day the tree asks the girl to come play and the response was I want to play with toys and the girl ask the tree does you have money the tree responded to the girl no I don't, but you can pick all the apples you want the girl said thank you Mr. apple tree you are such a great help to me the girl was so excited she took as many apples as possible she could leave and never showed up for a while well within months the girl came back, and the tree ask the girl to come play the tree was so excited to see the girl she responded again to the tree no I can't I have to work for my family for shelter she said Mr. tree can you help me the tree said you can chop off my branches to build a home, so the girl did so she

Oh, Mr. tree thank you so much so she chopped off the branches to build the home she left again came back the tree asked her to play again, and the girl said I'm so sad and lonely and that day way very hot the girl said I'm getting older can you help me with a boat so I can go sailing to relax myself the tree said cut my trunk off and that's what she did and again she left this time it was some years that had passed by the girl came back she was very old, and the tree seen her coming the tree told the girl I just don't have anything for you anymore no more apples for you no more.

I have no teeth no trunk for you to even climb anymore so the tree to the girl I am old the girl stated to the tree I don't need much now just a place to rest I am tired after all these years the girl said I have taken from you Mr. tree and not one time did you say no the tree said we grew up together like family and now my child my old roots are good to lean on and rest and the girl sat down beside the tree with tears in her eyes and the tree smiled with tears and now at the end of the day the moral of the story is that children are the trees and your parents when you were young, we played loved you held you feed you talked with you rocked you put you sleep and kept a smile on your face made sure harm didn't come to you and when you grew up and became adults you left the nest your parents then you flew back in like birds when you needed something or when you were in trouble no matter what your parents your parents say, or do we will always love you we will always be there to help you keep you on the right track when you are in trouble not happy going through something we as parents try to make you happy in this story you would think that this girl was being cruel to the tree but, that is how you children are treating us as parents to make a long story short you cannot continue to get over on your parents after all we did birth you and have done for you and then your statement is we owe you know my children's parents don't owe you nothing working on a situation can be only done biblical wisdom biblical wisdom doesn't like weeds in the flower bed, we must cultivate it through having our mind renewed being with believers and believers and hearing the word go as a parent in such situation we must keep growing as believer now for the parents who is hurting today if your heart is in shred this is for it was placed on my heart to tell you this, I don't know who you are, or what you're going through but we've all been there in some form or fashion, and I hope you find what you're looking for in these words it really hurt.

And I know it do it's like someone has took a cheese grater to your heart and left you the shreds I don't pretend to know what no one is going through I it knows it can be difficult when you have that as issue with heartache disappointment betrayal heavy decisions each parents have a different problem each one of us has something different that attempt to smile through every morning some days are better than others some days you wake up and think ok I can do this your mind is clear your heart is steady, and you feel ok to laugh you see a glimmer of hope and promises that you can cling to for the moment and there are some days you wake up wondering just how much more can you take before you absolutely crumble in tears and shattered in pieces to me it seems like now the burdened and the heavy load and the saddening and pain just continue to weight you down God let me know that I was going to be ok children are children and they will disappoint you and break you and break your heart after all as parents we have been broken and hurt in way adult children doesn't realize that parents hurt too but listen look at the intently words that are supposed to hear today there is one who want ever to hurt you or leave you lonely and that's our father in heaven God will never leave us, and he will never forsake us God will never break our heart or betray us or lie to us our God is a very understanding God my GODMY GOD he knows our hearts he knows the very ones that hurt us our God knows how to mend our broken hearts God will fill our wounds that are left open when our children shattered it when our wounds are left open by a cheese grater and God knows how to protects us as parents in ways others will just leave you wanting our God is a miracle maker a joy giver when things are impossible lost, hopeless children spinning out of control, feeling unwanted.

God is always there to pick us up when we are weak, he is strong when we feel tired, he is relentless when we feel broken, he is whole I just want to let all parents know that whatever we are going through something if we just step away and step down and let Jesus hold you and put the problem in his hand and let God fill up all those spaces in us heart from the damages our children put us through in thinking we owe them God will and he can fill those voided spaces and he will find piece for us in his present.

God will also give us our joy in his never ending love if you would just immerse yourself in God words that will be your lamp to your feet if you would just put one foot in front of the other and follow where he has led you as a parent then you will know in in your heart that God is leading you it's going to be ok this is not to say pain will be over or that he might be leading you through a path that will be difficult it may require a different road it may require you to cut all ties and losses and neither of these option will be easy it may be your season of healing and grief that requires you to find a result but parents know this we are never along GOD is always by us in every step of the way if you would just trust and follow and pursue forgive let it go move on cry when you must just scream then breathe we as parents must keep our heads and our hopes love continually and when you do these things and recover you will know that everything is going to be ok God will bring us through in all our storms that we may face as parents with our children we need the revelation the word from God and his promises to cling on to him I want to give all adults a word of wisdom that is what I do best I chose to pass on this not to my children but to whoever read this book I've learned over the years who would know better and whether you listen or not or even listen to would you listen to our parents meaning your grandparents perhaps these words of wisdom can set the intention to teach you parents are not your jobs not your possession find your passion look for what inspire you and do it pursue it with all your heart you may well find a way stop complaining and make your own decision for yourself instead of running to your parents to make your decision for yourself your decision is for your parents whatever you want in life you must want it for you and not what your parents have you also have to be grateful for your parents if they are still in this world.

Acknowledge your parents why they are still here and acknowledge them when they are gone you must learn the lesson for yourself and when thing change the world is changing you must get back up and find your way because parents have taught you many valuable lessons in life and by leading this life by the grace of God we have led you to the fullest after a period of eighteen years.

Your parent will tell you that they have devoted all their time and energy into you raising you now that you have become an adult you should start realizing it and realize how blessed you have parents and just be careful how you treat or talk to your parent there is a God that sits up high and looks down low and remember you may have to give accountable to authorities down here on earth but just remember you will have to give accountable to our almighty GODABOVE life is too short the bible explain that life is like breath here one moment, gone the next.

It also describes human life is like a flower again, here for a short while, then gone so the next time you say or think parent owe you. You need to remember that we gave your life that PARENTS DON'T OWE you nothing whether responsible or not parents make decision to bring children into this world who are dependent on them for many years. parents want to provide for their children they long to give them a stable environment educational opportunities nourishing meals but sometimes this well - intention deserves to backfires as a parent I had to do lot of steal away so if you don't know what I'm talking about when I say steal away is that I had to I had to get away from those who was hurting me my children hurt me so bad didn't think they would be the one who put stumbling blocks in my pathway very sad to say.

But I still love them, it's just a lesson to be learned adults' children assumes that their parents would take up the responsibility forever and to make out ravenous request long after they have left home the lack of clarify in the financial relationship between parent and adults children perhaps they paid for college degrees or other financial they have process the truth is that parents don't owe their grown children nothing or shall I say anything once that adult child has finished high school the financial pipe line dried up now knowing how to deal with the children sense of entitlement as a parent as a parent you have to tell yourself.

I've already done my dues as a parents you have to draw a line between you as a parent and the child you have to let them know it is their turn and they have to be self-sufficient as parent's mothers and parents have to demonstrates with a willingness on the behalf of the children. those same children you have raised and catered to and those same children you made happy is the same children that turns on you after the financial is removed from them so as a parent and overly concerned as a parent and the relationship with their adult children looking like I don't want to do nothing to hurt or damage their self-esteem as a mother that could say I don't want the adult child to be mad at me to that adult child looking at the parent and holding that parent responsible for their action and their emotional fragilities.

I just want to let these children know something don't wait to give respect your parents I just want them to know that want they are going it will be too late to cut up then I'm not just talking to my children I'm talking but anyone who disrespect their parents and thing the owe them something all children better make peace with parents not just your family but with your almighty lord cause one of these days you are sure going to have to meet your maker so please don't wait until it is too late in how you treat your parent I just all kid to know don't be like that that rich man in the bible.

They tell me Lazarus layer there begging he kept right on begging at the rich man gate the story tells me that when that rich man died he lifted up his eyes and that's when he prayed but then it was too late that's why I'm giving this message to the adult children honor your parents don't let it be too late before your parents leave this word because you don't want to be the one to watch as the roll your parent down the isle of the church it's no need to cry then because it will be too late when your there tongue have been glued to the root of their mouth it will be too late and their heart has stopped beating it's too late when the blood has stooping pumping blood from on vein to another somebody woke up looked down on your parents called their name.

And just couldn't answer you know that is too late so don't it be too late how you has treated your parents so don't let this be you treating your parents bad or thinking they owe you something they don't you have to think before as an adult I have learned so much as I continue my journey as a parent the only thing I wanted to do is be a parent to my children and make sure they are on the right pathway but it is what it is all I wanted to is to save them from harm but it so much a parent can do when you do all you can do as a parent and the adult backlash at you and talk against you and totally disrespected it's very sad and very sad and painful as a parent you wish so many things you could have teach that child before they walk out their home when they become an age all I wanted to do is teach them as a parent you can learn so much as a child becoming most parents would rank their parents among the most important and closest relationship in their lives but how many of these relationships are rooted in feeling of guilt for being cared for as adult children versus a genius feeling of love and respect. I had to forgive of how they were trying to ruin my life. It was the day bearing the fruit of betrayal.

It was the day of lying tongues and compromised   courts it was the day of brutal beating of vicious bloodletting it was the day of creaming and cursing and anger tyrants it was the day of violence on the heels of rejection it is the day of stark lioness in the wake of feeling friends it is the day of dismal darkness thunder and earthquakes it is the day of human arrogance and folly a Godforsaken day in God himself was killed as he submitted himself to the hands of his enemies it was the day beyond all others so it was like a day of all others, it is a day in our own certain way. I know that there are bad days and that is common in the world that is cynical observation. It is an honest one and so in many regards the similarities to order on things that Jesus endured are very much like those that I have often experience the God dimension suffering transcends our understanding just as it has transformed our lives the dynamics of the human Experience are often painfully approximate the epistle to the Philippians refer to it as the fellowship of His suffering {3: 10} and that is exactly what Jesus summoned to discovered in answering his call Take up your Cross and follow Me {matt. 16:24}. His call isn't an idealistic notion; it is practical pathway. It is our savior call to discipleship the call to take my yoke upon you and learn from me...... and you will find rest for your soul" {matt. 11:29. In other words the most final terms, discipleship is the call first and most necessarily to receive the forgiveness and the salvation afforded there alone by God great love we are not to remain solely as forgiven penitents we are called to grow as our father sons and daughters to serve to learn the master devotion and all the growth by the way we handle life blessing but by the way we live and how our adult children live through their bad days.

Now I know the bad day we all have bad days and bad days happen to everyone the come more often then we think we deserve and they sometimes last much longer than we think we can stand the reason every one needs Jesus to lean on we need Jesus to have a framework for processing the bad days and his word to direct us let us run with endurance the race that is set before us looking unto Jesus the author and the finisher of our faith who for the joy that was set before him endure the cross (heb.12:1-2).

Adults children that are experiencing bad days then you have apply to the lord word you have to call on the lord not to commiserate over agonies but you has to find companionship and direction you know the human pain and the problem is focus here all of the suffering all the rejection all of the painfulness all of the exhaustion all of the misunderstanding lioness all of the death all of these are the wisdom and understanding with all faith hope and love and it the love most of all that we are summoned to look upon Jesus and to expressly study the way the lord will provide the good days to come to us for the joy that was set before him he endured the cross and that explains to us both the where and the why are we to look the where brings us the cross to listen to his word spoken the day and the why is to find hope are especially told his endurance that bad day would be nourished by the joy waiting beyond it his promise to each of us is no less no less than spoken to a band of exiles.

I know the thoughts that I think towards you, say the lord, thoughts of peace and not of evil, to give you a future and of hope.

Then you will call upon me and go and pray to me and I will listen to you. And you will seek me and find me when you search for me with all your heart. I will be found by you says the lord, and I will bring you back from your captivity {Jer 29:11-14} as a parent and having an adult child that was living at home and you know that you are not along it seems like they leave home and come back and want to set themselves up to live independently they move out of the home and think they can just come back in as they feel like it just like they have never moved out of the home and they it's like they expect us as parents to take care of them and their needs and they are starting to feel resentful and frustrated as a mother you can only and actually make a career out of earning income from the parent by working the emotional system.

In today's world I look at how society has changed its views and approached to us as parents over the little of the generations the culture has increasingly encouraged to do what we can for our children in other words society has changed and moved from caring for our children to caretaking and as a result us as parents find themselves solving problems for the children long into adulthood. The question how this this happen in today's world children are usually born out of emotional wants or needs many wants to share the bond of having children and experiencing joy the picture of becoming a family we see having a child is part of Gods plan or sharing a spiritual experience you know teens that are becoming into adults believe that once they come into adulthood and move out of the home with their parents and then mess their life up come back home and try to put a twist on their parents like I need you to take care of me and get me back on my feet we are parents and we want our children to be happy confident and secure we hate to see them suffer and we as parents try to help and we try to cause the pain way in reality we as parent would want to go through pain yourself than to watch our children go through it.

As we can recall and remember our own childhood pain as we watch our children struggle to find their way in the world. We empathize with our children. How many children are held back in life because they feel obliged to remain obedient to an authorization parent well into adulthood. As a mother that has cause a stir on the platform by asking with parents proclaiming that parents don't owe their children nothing, we as parents don't owe them anything it is so wrong for children try to make their parents fill guilty for thinking they owe them something the things was just setting boundaries with adult children.

Many times in my life as a parent I did all I could do what was right had to lay awake many nights all nights and I had to call on the lord to help me get through all I had to do is hold on and let the lord fight my battles I had to let the lord continue to be in charge of my life I had to go on and let the lord continue to have charge in my life I'm writing this book that was place on my heart by the lord saying to my children do let it be too late. I knew that got will take care of me my children have failed to hear the message the message was heavy for them I'm writing this book telling my children don't leave your parent now today I'm worry about my soul I had to look unto the lord and continue to go on.

God is in charge of my life it now makes no different what has been said and done I want to let my children know that God is still of my life and I'm going to continue to stand on his word I use to lay awake at night thinking about all they have done to me I had to keep my hand in God hand all I had to do is not worried. Adult children like I say we as parents don't owe you nothing tell you the truth you children you owe us purely virtue a relationship of raising all regarding the choice to procreate the answer as it would appear to me as a mother is looking at it cursorily would   be that their as a mother there is no inherent obligation the adult child has no choice nor any influence upon the decision in I have made to procreate:; in other words as a parent do for you after eighteen years is out of pure love respect it and be thankful.

Now I understand why some parent disowned their children you can push a parent so far, to be so disrespectful and take advantage of them for so long before they can take it. Hers the reality as a parent I'm getting older not younger but older for another generation to come in and the older I get the wiser the older I get the time is pushing faster like the clock it's all about time as a parent I will not be here always and I won't be here forever instead adult children being a constant source of stress and drama you children should be a light load for me as a parent as a parent I have already done and did my duties and took time out to be the parent that I am to raising you as a single parent it's all right to ask for a accept help feed you clothes you kept it to act as if we are somehow owed something is dysfunctional and manipulative it is time for you to grow up just because I am your mom.

I'm going to love you forever no matter what – you can't treat me just any old kind of way and think you can get away with it matter to me cause I birth you brought you into this world feed you clothes you kept roof over your heads and protected you to the best of my ability don't never treat the person who loves you the most the worst don't take me for granted I may not let you see but your shortness impatience and harsh words make me steal away and when I say steal way I'm referring to I have to fold my arms and shake my head go to a quiet place and cry my heart hurts too and my heart hurts for understanding why I feel so angry.

I will not argue with you but I will always love you it doesn't matter how old you are I will still love you and it doesn't matter how old I am as a mother I will always treasure you as a parent you only have one mother and when she is gone you will never find another one to replace her or you will never find another mother so adults children watch your thoughts and watch your words watch your action because one day it may be the toughest time in your life and stop saying that parents don't owe you nothing.

Proverbs 13:1 -25

A wise son heeds his father's instruction, but the mocker does not respond to rebukes. From the fruit of their lips people enjoy good things, but the unfaithful have an appetite for violence. Those who guard their lips preserves their lives, but those who speak rashly will come to ruin. A sluggard's appetite is never filled, but the desire of the diligent are fully satisfied the righteous hates what is false but the wicked makes themselves a stench and bring shame on themselves. Righteousness guards the person of integrity but the wickedness overthrows the sinner one person pretends to be rich, yet has nothing and another pretends to be poor, yet has great wealth. A person riches may ransom their life, but the poor cannot respond to threatening rebates the light of the righteous may ransom their life but the righteously shines brightly but the lamp of the wicked is snuffed out where is strife, there is pride, but wisdom is found in those who takes advise dishonest money dwindles away but whoever gathers money little by little it grows hopes deferred makes the heart sick but a longing fulfilled is a tree of life whoever scorns instruction will pay for it, but whoever respects a command is rewarded the teaching of the wise is a fountain of life turning a person from the snares of death good judgment wins favors, but the way of the unfaithful leads to destruction all who are prudent act with knowledge, but fools expose their folly a wicked messenger falls into trouble, but a trustworthy envoys brings healing whoever disregarded discipline comes to poverty and shame, but whoever heed correction is honored a longing fulfilled is sweet to the soul, but fools detest turning from evil. Walk with the wise and become wise, for a companion of fools suffers harm trouble pursues the sinner, but the righteous with good things an unplowed field produced food for the poor, but justice sweeps it away whoever spares the rod hates their children, but the one loves their children is careful to discipline them, the righteous eat to their hearts content, but the stomach of the wicked goes hungry. Children obeying their parents is a direct command from the lord, Ephesian 6:1 says, children, obey your parents in the lord for this is right." in this verse, obeying one's parents cannot separate from horning one's parent Ephesian 6 continues, honor you mother and father and a mother which is the first command with a promise so that it may go well with you and you may enjoy long life on earth. Honor means children are to have attitude of respect towards their parents. A child obedience to their parents is to be done with an attitude of honor. Obedience with a bad attitude does not conform to the command it may bring challenging for some children to learn to obey their parents. A strong will certainly makes it harder for some children's than others. there is no good reason for this command proverbs 13:1 teaches that those who listen to their parents will regain wisdom:" a wise son heeds from his father instruction, but a mocker does not respond to rebates. "gods design is for his children's to learn respect home, and they will respect others when they leave home even Jesus, though he was the son of god, he obeys his earthly parents and as a results, he grew into wisdom in Luke 2:51:52 the bible also says that that children who are not discipline or who fail to learn to obey their parents will be much worse off in life. Proverbs 29-15 reminds us "the rod and reproof give wisdom, but a child left to himself brings shame to their mother. "proverbs 29"17 also says," discipline your son, and he will give you rest: he will give delight to your heart". As children have responsibilities to obey their parents also has responsibilities to instruct their children without frosting the, as unowned in Ephesian 6:4 fathers, do not   exasperate your children to break it down or in so many words which mean the discipline of a child should not be punitive is nature but corrective. Parents are not to make their children pay but are to discipline them so they are being disciplined parents also have a responsibility to bring up their children to know and love the lord. the primary of a child places it to be taught the faith and to be formed in the faith is at home. This is seen in Ephesians 6:4 bring them up in the training and instruction of the lord.; even if the parent are not falling god`s command directed toward them about disciplining a child correctly children still has responsibilities to honor and obey your parents when a child leaves home, while they are independent of their parents as adult children, they still have a responsibility to honor your father and mother, one of the ten commandments exodus 20:12 honor your father and mother, that your days may be long in the land of the lord God has given you. "this commandments doesn't just pertain to young children honoring adult parents but still instruct adult children about their responsibility to honor their aging parents as a general rule, the better children learn to honor respect there earthly father, the better they will learn to respect and obey and obeying the heavenly father the only appropriate reason for young to obey their parents is if parents instruct their children to do something that clearly goes against one of gods commands. In that case, children must obey God rather than man in acts 5:29. You know parents want to give advice all the time because they want to protect you from making the mistake that we have made or that someone has made that way, as a parent will understand how you feel and then they will have a chance to explain things. Obedience to parents is important God promises train your child in a way he should go: and when he is old, he will not depart from it" proverbs 22:6 Parents, who see one of their children hit the fan, often have a hard time appreciating this verse. In fact, as the homeschool movement ages there are more and more parents claiming the verse does not mean what it says, because it didn't hold true in their experience. Not here is some reason a child is lost to the world and how parents caused it to happen without even trying I say without trying because when adult children turn out poorly as many do parents are at a loss as to why it is always unexpected certainly unplanned an eighteen year old is unthankful and rebellious walks around like the family is his emery and he has been enslaved and abused by them his whole life anger is his first respond to everything and to nothing. So I'm going to let you know how adult children's come to ruin us end without their parents exerting any effort or attention to the process at all in fact that is the first step toward sabotaging your adult children's future no effort and no attention.

I've learned in raising my children are like plants growing everyday while they are young they need regular attention and direction and lots of children's turn out poorly as mint do parents are at a loss to why.

Let me say this I planted a garden every year and about half of the time I wait too long to stake my tomatoes a small plant doesn't need staking and I tell myself I will stake them before it becomes critical.

But it may rain for an entire week, or I get busy doing something else and can't get around to it the plant gets so big so big the stems fall on the ground when the leaves of a tomato plant are exposed to the soil they quickly develop disease. When the fruit touches the ground it will rot about the time it should be getting ripe. This year I had a second late patch that I intended to stake but waited too long I finally staked them but too late to prevent the disease. It is not what I did; it is what I didn't do that spoiled the crop so it is with children they need constant pruning and fertilizing and training to grow up instead of down to reach for blue skies instead of crawling along the ground so the worst thing you can do for your children is just ignore them and allow nature to take its course children need admonition like a plant need fertilize making it available to the roots the smiles activate our admonition making it available to a soul of the child children raised right grow up right no exception it is Gods certain promise proverbs 22:6 the children that came into the world disciplined and wise and willing to deny their impulses for the greeted good we could just leave them to expression but every parent knows better all children come to us innocent but falling they are hedonistic self-indulging in their national state left to themselves they will bring mothers to shame proverbs 29:15. Adult are supposed to be mature enough to choose the virtuous path and do what they ought to do even if is contrary to their desires. The characters something that you are not born with it has to be developed and children don't have characters unless they are properly trained children do not see the need for self-denial or self-restraint they feel desire and they do what feels good. So if a parent does nothing their children will become quite in the dark arts of self-arts of self-indulgence therefore parents must contain their children to right behavior in time their moral understanding will developed and they will begin to choose good even when it is contrary to their carnal desires characters is in formed and as training continue s to grow stronger until he matures into an adult hardly anything is more heartbreaking than having one or more adult children simple disappearing from our lives for no apparent reason yes , it seems inconceivable but it happens a lot more often than we think the cruel grief of such a loss is often more than any of us parents can bear. Even the idea of such losses sounds absurd and can send most of us packing the sadness and possible shame we bear is not something we discuss idly with fellow parents many of whom are enjoying seemingly the connection of their parents money it sends shivers down my spine to know that our children are alive but they are not seeing us the trauma from losing our children in this way can worse that we are losing our children to death such as pain that affects our relationship but in general the adult children's choose not to listen to us as parents. There are other reasons why us as parents loses words over such losses they are simple incomprehensible. The unfortunate truth is that is that they cannot explain why they do the thing they do to hurt us as parents there is no reason obvious reason for it the most that I can see is the lack of their own explanation for why our kids just drift from us and their own lives most they hate the burden that they have brought to themselves and they tries to put it on the parents now they suffer and now they can hardly bear and are very reluctant to let the cat out of the bag regarding the wayward so when they damage their lives and tries to damage their parents and they see they can't now they want to isolate themselves and not it's the unspeakable to silence not let's be clear it is indeed not normal for adult children's to do things to hurt their parents adult children do in fact have a natural drive and responsivity to acknowledge their parents in this book I'm writing as a parent just want others parents know they are not alone even though it is painful of how adults children treat us we still have to continue to trust in the lords and we have to continue to pray for them and we as parents have to continue to keeping a moving. As adult children have twisted filial piety from "listen and be good to your parents" to "blind obedience to your parents." The problem is that raising a child is hard work; you're meant to give them love and support so they can build good habits growing up. What happens over the years of raising into an adult skip the hard work and just use filial piety to as a crutch to raising kids. "Your parents are always right" grows into "listen to me or else" and the train keeps going. The narcissism builds and the parents start thinking they really are the absolute moral authority, correct in everything. Then the mind warps, telling itself "If I'm the absolute moral authority, the kid should follow everything. They have goals they didn't achieve in life and want you to be better. parents truly love their kids, We Have Towards Our Parents When They Get Older.

Have you ever thought about the duties we have towards our parents when they get older I'm not talking about legal obligations (which there really aren't any)? I'm talking about the moral and ethical responsibilities. It's something that I've thought about a lot, especially after realizing just how many things our parents sacrifice to make our lives better when we're young. I truly believe we owe our parents when they reach their "golden" years. Have you ever thought about the duties we have towards our parents when they get older I'm not talking about legal obligations (which there really aren't any)? I'm talking about the moral and ethical responsibilities. It's something that I've thought about a lot, especially after realizing just how many things our parents sacrifice to make our lives better when we're young. truly I believe we owe our parents when they reach their "golden" years. Treat them with dignity and respect. First and foremost, treat your parents with the dignity and respect that they deserve. Nearly everything that follows below embodies that duty, but it's so important that it needs to be clearly stated upfront. Every single person on this earth, from the very young to the very old, deserves to be treated with dignity. While respect, on the other hand, is something that should be earned rather than given freely, I think we can all agree that our parents have more than earned it. Don't treat us like children. In our society, we tend to treat our elderly like children. If you don't believe me, the next time you go shopping or to a restaurant, pay attention to how clerks and servers talk to toddlers. Then, listen to the tone they use with elders. All too often, you'll find that it's the exact same tone. This is called "infantizing" them, Listen to them. Your parents spent, at a minimum, 18 years listening to you (although probably way beyond that). They patiently answered your 10,000 "why" questions when you were a toddler. They showed genuine interest in your utterly fascinating story a bug you saw on the playground in kindergarten. During your teen years, they listened to you complain (and complain and complain) about everything from unfair teachers to unjust curfews. Now, it's your turn to listen to them. Yes, even if they tell you the same story over and over. After all, how many times did they have to hear about that playground bug

We get so busy in our adult lives that we often forget to call home, much less visit regularly. It happens, and it doesn't mean you're a bad son or daughter.

Your parents know that you have a "life of your own" now. Shouldn't that life include them more, though Treat them with dignity and respect. Hebrews 2:1-4. Moms and dads are accustomed to dishing out advice. To try and guide a son or daughter through the narrow straights of life is part of the responsibility of a parent. Some guidance, if not heeded, will cost, but the price is not too severe. "Brush your teeth before you go to bed," mom says. If you don't take her advice, then you might have to suffer the sounds of a dentist's drill. Oh, it won't be a walk in the park, but you will get over it. "Be sure and write down all of your homework assignments," dad chimes in. If you fail to heed the advice, then you will probably make a bad grade. No big deal, right I mean you can make it up on the next test or maybe the teacher will let you do some work for extra credit. Some advice is far costlier if not taken seriously and applied to life. "Save yourself Don't allow yourself to get in a situation where your passions control you," mom tells her daughter, dad tells his son. If you fail to listen and heed the advice you won't need mom or dad to say, "I told you so." You will be reminded day-in and day-out of the decision you have made by the cries of a baby. "Don't do drugs and get drunk," dad tells you as you leave the house on Friday night.

If you think he is just an old man who doesn't want you to have any fun you may end up in jail, find yourself addicted to what will destroy you, or worse, in a body bag because of your failure to heed dad's advice. "Don't hang out with kids who lack character," mom and dad tell you over and over again. If you think your wisdom exceeds that of your father and you go ahead and make friends with the wrong crowd you could pay with the loss of your reputation. Parents accustomed to handing out advice.

They try and help get you through the world and get you to read the bible They try help reconcile when it comes to your life when it turns sour. They try and help people who've found themselves walking on the wild side, begin to walk on the Lord's side. They try and instill in others what is truly meaningful in life and what is nothing more than decoration. Teachers and coaches are quite proficient at offering advice to help young people become skilled at everything from history and biology to form tackling and free throws. They work on the little things, never overlook minor deficiencies, and praise a job well done. Advice comes to us from all angles. There are many, many counselors and advisor's preachers all around us who are willing to give us good counsel concerning things that really matter in life. If we will pay attention and heed the advice of those who truly want to help, those who are equipped to help us, then we can experience the benefits of wise counsel.

If we disregard the advice of others and try and go it alone then we are sure to find ourselves lost on the high seas of life, taking bad turns whenever we make a move, and wondering what has gone wrong. Among all of the counselors and teachers that are provided for us there is one bit of advice, that if we fail to take it seriously, if we take it too lightly, if we decide to get around to it one day – it will cost us everything. Disregarding the advice of the wise old sage of Hebrew lore will mean nothing less than utter despair and destruction. The consequences are real. The price is far too high to consider. To miss the ship would mean to miss everything of value, everything that is precious, and all that is priceless. Today, as we turn once again to the powerful book of Hebrews we find the most serious insight, the most pressing proposition, and the most priceless promise that will ever come our way. I pray that if you have slept through services in the past, or never paid attention before, that today you will heed the advice of the ages of wisdom and consider the cost of letting the promise drift right by you. Let's take a look at Hebrews 2:1-4. 1We must pay more careful attention, therefore, to what we have heard, so that we do not drift away. 2For if the message spoken by angels was binding, and every violation and disobedience received its just punishment, 3how shall we escape if we ignore such a great salvation

This salvation, which was first announced by the Lord, was confirmed to us by those who heard him. 4Godalso testified to it by signs, wonders and various miracles, and gifts of the Holy Spirit distributed according to his will. (Hebrews 2:1-4 NIV) As we turn our attention back to the book of Proverbs we move into the fathers fifth lesson for his son. This lesson is unique from the standpoint that it is really a lesson that Solomon's dad, King David, had shared with him when he was young. Now Solomon is passing it on to his son. As we get into our Scripture for this morning we will see that Solomon is urging his son to pursue and acquire wisdom at all costs. Solomon heeded his father's advice when he was a young man.

He is a wonderful example of how godly wisdom will bless our lives, protect our steps, and empower us with insight, leadership, and discernment that is beyond our abilities. When Solomon first became King, as the successor of his father King David, he was visited by Godin a dream one night. God told Solomon, ask for anything you want and I will give it to you. Turn with me to 1 Kings 3 and let's read what took place. 5At Gibeon the LORD appeared to Solomon during the night in a dream, and God said, ask for whatever you want me to give you. 6Solomon answered, you have shown great kindness to your servant, my father David, because he was faithful to you and righteous and upright in heart. You have continued this great kindness to him and have given him a son to sit on his throne this very day. 7Now, O LORD my God, you have made your servant king in place of my father David. But I am only a little child and do not know how to carry out my duties. 8Your servant is here among the people you have chosen, a great people, too numerous to count or number. 9So give your servant a discerning heart to govern your people and to distinguish between right and wrong.

For who is able to govern this great people of yours 10The Lord was pleased that Solomon had asked for this. 11So God said to him, since you have asked for this and not for long life or wealth for yourself, nor have asked for the death of your enemies but for discernment in administering justice, 12I will do what you have asked. I will give you a wise and discerning heart, so that there will never have been anyone like you, nor will there ever be. 13Moreover, I will give you what you have not asked for both riches and honor so that in your lifetime you will have no equal among kings. 14And if you walk in my ways and obey my statutes and commands as David your father did, I will give you a long life. (1 Kings 3:5-14 NIV) The same story is repeated in 2 Chronicles 1:7-10.

What an incredible experience it must have been for Solomon to have God show up and say, anything you ask and it is yours! What would we ask God for if we were given a blank check for many of us it would be exactly what God told Solomon He would give him because he did not ask for them wealth, a long life, and vengeance against Solomon's enemies. For most people today we would not hesitate to ask God to make us rich, to give us good health, to make us famous, or to give us a long and prosperous life. Yet how many people do you know who have these things and they still are not content, they still cannot find the happiness that they long for in life These things were given to Solomon, but they were not his priority. Solomon desired Gods wisdom first and foremost. Solomon, as a young man, was a great example of a person who had their priorities in place. Solomon, as an older man, is a tragic example of what can happen if we allow our pursuit of wisdom, our relationship with God, to become a past time. We can't afford to arrive at the conclusion that we have become wise because of our past track record. Neither can we become so busy that we put our pursuit of God and His wisdom on the back burner while we pursue lesser things.

As an older man Solomon's priorities got shifted, he was led astray by the very things that he counseled his son to avoid. Solomon's pursuits ruined his life and led to the destruction of the nation. The lessons that were passed along to Solomon by his father, David, were forgotten and the lives of many were affected as a result. Our pursuit of godly wisdom must be a life-long passion, a first priority, or we will suffer the consequences of living a foolish, misguided life. As we come to our Scripture for today in Proverbs 4:1-9 we need to hear the wisdom of the ages being passed from generation to generation. At the same time, we need to hear the call to pursue this wisdom with all of our heart and then pass it on. In Proverbs 4:1-9 we read, 1 Listen, my sons, to a father's instruction; pay attention and gain understanding. 2 I give you sound learning, so do not forsake my teaching. 3 When I was a boy in my father's house, still tender, and an only child of my mother, 4 he taught me and said, lay hold of my words with all your heart; keep my commands and you will live. 5 Get wisdom, get understanding; do not forget my words or swerve from them. 6 Do not forsake wisdom, and she will protect you; love her, and she will watch over you. 7 Wisdom is supreme; therefore, get wisdom. Though it cost all you have, get understanding. 8 Esteem her, and she will exalt you; embrace her, and she will honor you. 9 She will set a garland of grace on your head and present you with a crown of splendor. (Proverbs 4:1-9 NIV) As I mentioned earlier, this is the fathers fifth lesson given to his son on the importance of wisdom for his life. If, when we read the Scripture, you felt like we were reading some of the same material that we have studied earlier then you are exactly right. Repetition is a key to learning. We need the same lessons over and over again if we are going to maintain our focus and passion in seeking to learn and obey godly wisdom. The foundation of each of these lessons is the importance of wisdom, specifically the wisdom of God for living life, experiencing the contentment and happiness that only God can bring, and for protecting us from the destruction that accompanies a life lived foolishly, in contradiction to godly wisdom.

With each lesson Solomon desires to lay a foundation, the foundation of the wisdom of God, as well as direct the lessons to situations and scenarios that the young man will experience as he grows and matures. Let's turn our attention to verse 1. Read along with me. 1 Listen, my sons, to a father's instruction; pay attention and gain understanding. (Proverbs 4:1 NIV) I want us to notice something very important within this verse. Solomon urges his sons to pay attention and gain understanding. This is such an important phrase for us to understand because God's lessons come to us each and every day if we are paying attention. For many of us, we have to learn the same lessons over and over again because we are not paying attention. The word that is used here in verse 1 for pay attention is found 8 times in the book of Proverbs. There is no question that the father is urging his son to learn from the lessons that are being offered to him. The Hebrew word for pay attention means, to hear, be attentive, or heed. The word conveys to us the activity of hearing and obeying. To pay attention to God means that we not only hear what He has to say, but we follow hearing with obedience. There are other places in the Hebrew Bible where we find this same word. Let me show you a couple of places where the word appears so that we can understand the two pronged meaning of the word. Turn with me to 1 Samuel 15:22-23 and well see our first example. Saul was the first king of Israel. While he was king he was instructed to attack the Amalekites because of the way they treated the Israelites when they came out of slavery in Egypt. Saul was instructed to destroy everything, but he didn't follow God's instructions. Saul spared King Agag and the best of the livestock, but that was not what God had told him to do. When Saul was confronted he made excuses about why did other than what God had told him to do. He was going to use the livestock as a sacrifice to God, but that was not what God had told him to do. Now, in 1 Samuel 15:22-23 we read about God's response to what Saul's excuses. Read along with me. 22But Samuel replied: Does the LORD delight in burnt offerings and sacrifices as much as in obeying the voice of the LORD to obey is better than sacrifice, and to heed is better than the fat of rams. 23 For rebellion is like the sin of divination, and arrogance like the evil of idolatry. Because you have rejected the word of the LORD, he has rejected you as king. (1 Samuel 15:22-23 NIV) The word heed here is the same Hebrew word that we find in Proverbs 4:1. Obedience is better than religious rituals, obedience is better than pious excuses, and it is better than giving God lip service, but allowing our hearts to be far from Him. The second place that I want to show you this morning is found in Isaiah 48:17-19. The people of God had not listened and there was a big price to pay for their unwillingness to listen to God. They did what they wanted, they did what they thought was best for them, but they did not do what God desired for them. God says, 17 This is what the LORD says your Redeemer, the Holy One of Israel: I am the LORD your God, who teaches you what is best for you, who directs you in the way you should go. 18 If only you had paid attention to my commands, your peace would have been like a river, your righteousness like the waves of the sea. 19 Your descendants would have been like the sand, your children like its numberless grains; their name would never be cut off nor destroyed from before me. (Isaiah 48:17-19 NIV) Notice that some of the very things that are promised in Proverbs 4, for those who live according to God's wisdom, are mentioned here in Isaiah 48. God says in Isaiah 48 that if they had only listened their peace would have been like a river, their righteousness like the waves of the sea, their descendants would have been more numerous than the grains of sand, and they would not be destroyed. That is if they would have listened, if they would have paid attention, if they would have obeyed. Can you see how important it is for us to pay attention to God when He gives us lessons in how to live wisely, how to live godly lives, regardless of what popular opinion would have us do, or what conventional wisdom would suggest.

Remember that this lesson is being taught not in the halls of higher learning, not in some prestigious Ivy League school, or any school for that matter. These lessons of wisdom are being taught by a father and mother to their son. Later on they became a kind of curriculum for the training of young people, but they originated in the home.

I'm so glad that all of us can gain from studying these life lessons, but we must remember that the first nine chapters are put in the mouths of parents and offered to their children. Let's take a look at the kind of relationship that was shared by the parents with their children. Read along with me in verse 3. 3 When I was a boy in my father's house, still tender, and an only child of my mother (Proverbs 4:3 NIV) In Proverbs 4 we can get a snapshot of the Hebrew home. The son is tender The word means, soft, weak, or tender. The word paints a picture for us of a child who is vulnerable, his character is pliable, moldable, and he is vulnerable to negative influences. Isn't that true of young people still to this day There are so many influences, so many shaping forces present in our society that will, without a thought, bend them and twist them into a mangled mess if there is not someone to intervene. This is nothing new my friends. Young hearts have always been easily influenced, but Godin His Providence has supplied gracious but firm hands by way of a loving mother and father to shape the child according to God's Word and His ways.

So we have the nature of children. Young, easily influenced, desperately needing the guiding and shaping hands of their parents to instill within them the wisdom and discernment necessary to avoid the pitfalls and destruction of life lived apart from the authority of God. We also have here in verse 3 an insight into the demeanor and style of training given by the parents. Solomon says that he was an only child of my mother. In writing this Solomon says that he was Bathsheba's only child. Bathsheba had a child before Solomon was born, but he had died when he was an infant. Along with pointing out that he was an only child Solomon is trying to convey an additional message to his readers. Let me show you what I am talking about. The Hebrew word that is used here means only one, solitary, or unique.

It is the uniqueness that I want to focus on for a moment. In Genesis 22:9-12 we read about the story of God calling Abraham to take his only son Isaac up to Mt. Moriah and to offer him as a sacrifice there. Read along with me. When they reached the place God had told him about, Abraham built an altar there and arranged the wood on it. He bound his son Isaac and laid him on the altar, on top of the wood. 10Then he reached out his hand and took the knife to slay his son. 11But the angel of the LORD called out to him from heaven, Abraham! Abraham! Here I am, he replied. 12Do not lay a hand on the boy, he said. Do not do anything to him. Now I know that you fear God, because you have not withheld from me your son, your only son. (Genesis 22:9-12 NIV) Now we know that Isaac wasn't Abraham's only son. He had a son born before Isaac, Ishmael, who was born to Hagar.

Isaac was Abraham's only son born to Sarah, but he was his unique son in that he was the son promised by God Whom God would use to accomplish His purposes in redemptive history. The same word is used by David in Psalms 22:20 and Psalms 35:17, but here the word is translated as precious. Turn with me to these verses and let's take a look. 20 Deliver my life from the sword, my precious life from the power of the dogs. (Psalm 22:20 NIV) 17 O Lord, how long will you look on Rescue my life from their ravages, my precious life from these lions. (Psalms 35:17 NIV)

This word precious is a beautiful description to show us the meaning of the word found in Proverbs 4:3. Solomon's mother cherished her son, he was unique to her, and she loved him with a special love. We who are parents today need to view our children, each of our children, as unique creations of God. We don't raise kids with a parenting manual bought from Barnes and Noble, with a cookie cutter approach handed down by some authority, or according to Dr. Spock or Dr. Phil. We are to prayerfully consider the uniqueness of each of our children and encourage, teach, love, and discipline them accordingly. God's Word is our textbook in instilling within our children discernment, wisdom, and a moral foundation.

Along with these our children need to learn to pray in order to know the how of applying Gods Word to the situations and struggles they will face in life. We are much more than coaches or reservoirs of truth We are lovers of our kids. Each of our children needs to feel that they are their mom and dad's beloved the only child, precious in their mom or dad's eyes, rather than just another child. As we move on in our study I want to shift our focus from the nature of a young person and the demeanor of the parents to the urgent call of the parents to get wisdom. Read along with me from Proverbs 4:4-5. 4 he taught me and said, lay hold of my words with all your heart; keep my commands and you will live. 5 Get wisdom, get understanding; do not forget my words or swerve from them. (Proverbs 4:4-5 NIV) The dad says to lay hold of his counsel to get wisdom, to get understanding. What does it mean to lay hold of something How do you grab on to lessons I'm so glad you asked? The Hebrew word for lay hold is tamak The word means to grasp, hold, or to be held. The King James Version of the Bible translates the word, retain. Let me show you some of the places where the word appears in other places in the Old Testament and you can get a better idea of how to hold on to wisdom. 8 My soul clings to you; your right hand upholds me. (Psalm 63:8 NIV) 21 For a man's ways are in full view of the LORD, and he examines all his paths. 22 The evil deeds of a wicked man ensnare him; the cords of his sin hold him fast. (Proverbs 5:21-22 NIV) To lay hold is an action that takes place, not a mind-set. You can see from the two verses we just read that we are faced with a choice either we will lay hold of wisdom which is truly clinging to the Lord and His Word or sin will lay hold of us and hold us in its grasp. There is no other choice. Practically speaking, for you and me to lay hold of wisdom we must lay hold of God's Word. Read it, pray over it, meditate upon it, and recite it to ourselves throughout the day. It is truly remarkable how God will bring His Word to mind when we face situations in life.

Let's take a look at the last part of our lesson. Read along with me from Proverbs 4:6-9.

6 Do not forsake wisdom, and she will protect you; love her, and she will watch over you. 7 Wisdom is supreme; therefore, get wisdom. Though it cost all you have, get understanding. 8 Esteem her, and she will exalt you; embrace her, and she will honor you. 9 She will set a garland of grace on your head and present you with a crown of

splendor. (Proverbs 4:6-9 NIV)

For those who desire godly wisdom more than anything else there are benefits that they will enjoy that can't come in any other way. I want to mark these for us this morning. Take a look at these four verses with me and you can follow along.

Do not forsake wisdom
 She will protect you
Love her She will watch over you
Esteem her She will exalt you
Embrace her She will honor you.
She will set a garland of grace on your head and
present you with a crown of splendor

If we will not forsake wisdom, if we will love wisdom, esteem wisdom, and embrace wisdom then we are told that wisdom will protect us, watch over us, exalt us, honor us, and crown us with grace and splendor. What a wonderful promise! Some of you might be wondering if it is true Will God really protect us Don't you see people every day who are seeking after God that suffer Absolutely! As you go through Gods Word and read about the men and women who pour their hearts out in service to the Lord you will find men and women who suffered. Tears spotted Jeremiah's scroll as he wrote about his sufferings in Judah. Prison cell doors echoed in Paul's ears as he wrote to the Church in Philippi. David was on the run from King Saul, hiding in a cave, as he wrote the opening words of Psalm 57.

1 Have mercy on me, O God, have mercy on me, for in you my soul takes refuge. I will take refuge in the shadow of your wings until the disaster has passed. (Psalm 57:1 NIV) Stephen was stoned to death, Peter was crucified upside down, and do I even need to mention that the One who took off His royal robes of splendor and majesty to come and save us. He was beaten, mocked, His body ripped to shreds, and then nailed to a tree. So what kind of protection does wisdom provide How does wisdom watch over us Scripture teaches us that wisdom, obedience to God, is not a shield from suffering, but that it is a shield from sin and destruction. There are two ways that wisdom will protect us and watch over us. First, godly wisdom will protect us from falling into sin. If we will live according to God's Word then we will avoid so many heartaches that are brought about by living life as we want to live, by living life according to what we feel instead of by His Word. Godly wisdom will provide a way of escape for you and me. Take a look at 1 Corinthians 10:13 with me. 13No temptation has seized you except what is common to man. And God is faithful; he will not let you be tempted beyond what you can bear. But when you are tempted, he will also provide a way out so that you can stand up under it. (1 Corinthians 10:13 NIV) If you and I will live by God's wisdom, then, when sin knocks at our door, His wisdom will counsel us that destruction lies beyond the

enticing appeal of sin's offer.

The second way that wisdom will protect us and watch over us is that godly wisdom gives us the assurance that all of life has its purpose. This gives us great hope. We are not the victims of our situations; we are living under the watchful eye of our Sovereign God. Let me show you two instances of this protection against hopelessness, fear, and despair. In Psalm 23:4 David writes,

4 Even though I walk through the valley of the shadow of death, I will fear no evil, for you are with me; your rod and your staff, they comfort me. (Psalm 23:4 NIV) In Psalm 9 we learn that those who know, those who are intimately acquainted with the Lord will trust in Him rather than throw in the towel. Read along with me from Psalm 9:10. 10 Those who know your name will trust in you, for you, LORD, have never forsaken those who seek you. (Psalm 9:10 NIV) What is the key to unlocking the benefits of wisdom in our lives That's a great question. The key is found in verse 7.

7 Wisdom is supreme; therefore, get wisdom. Though it cost all you have, get understanding. (Proverbs 4:7 NIV) Though it costs you everything, get it! There is no price too high to pay get it! There is no sacrifice too great to make get it! Get it! When you are tired and weary get it! When you have bills to pay and you wonder if you are going to be able to make your rent get it! When your marriage is having problems and you think you would be better served doing something

else get it! When your friends entice you or your schedule is loaded with responsibilities don't neglect it, get it! Get it! Get wisdom! Gain understanding! You and I can get it by getting into His Word regularly, consistently, persistently, and with passion. Once you get it then pass it on. Oh how the world around us is yearning for truth, for something to be able to hold onto. Pass it on. Oh how our children are crying out for a foundation, for some stability, for some sense of purpose. Pass it on. Don't hold it to yourself pass it on. For you to ever come to know and walk in Gods wisdom you must first come to know Jesus Christ. John Piper has written such a powerful little paragraph about the need to know Jesus if we are ever going to come to know wisdom. He writes, Finally, there is one last, absolutely essential thing to do if you would "get wisdom": you must come to Jesus. He said to the people of his day, "The queen of the south will arise at the judgment with this generation and condemn it, for she came from the ends of the earth to hear the wisdom of Solomon, and behold something greater than Solomon is here" (Matthew 12:42). What an understatement. Greater than Solomon indeed! Solomon spoke God's wisdom. Jesus is the wisdom of God (1 Corinthians 1:24, 30). Others had spoken truth; he is the truth. Others had pointed the way to life; he is the way and the life (John 14:6). Others had given promises, but "all the promises of God find their yes in him" (2 Corinthians 1:20). Others had offered God's forgiveness; Jesus bought it by his death. Therefore, in him are "hid all the treasures of wisdom and knowledge" (Colossians 2:3). To know and love and follow this Jesus is to own the treasure of ultimate and eternal happiness. Therefore, the command, "Get wisdom" means first and foremost "Come to Jesus! Come to Jesus!" in whom are hid all the treasures of wisdom. (John Piper, Bethlehem Baptist Church, May 24, 1981)

Won't you welcome Him into your heart this morning Won't you bow before His throne of grace and mercy and cry out to the Lord this very day.

We receive reminders throughout our lives to pay attention – to our spouses, children, parents, teachers, employers, etc. The Bible also emphasizes the importance of paying attention. In this article, we are going to see what we are – and are not – to pay attention to and why it matters.

Pay Attention to These Things

To what we have heard – "For this reason we must pay much closer attention to what we have heard, so that we do not drift away from it" (Hebrews 2:1). "What we have heard" in this context does not necessarily mean what we were taught growing up. Instead, this is about what has been revealed by the apostles. Anyone who teaches something contrary to this "is to be accursed" (Galatians 1:8-

9). Therefore, this message is not going to change. So we are to "pay much closer attention" to it and grow spiritually, progressing from "the pure milk of the word" to the "solid food...for the mature" (1 Peter 2:2; Hebrews 5:13-14).

To the revelation of Christ – "So we have the prophetic word made more sure, to which you do well to pay attention as to a lamp shining in a dark place, until the day dawns and the morning star arises in your hearts" (2 Peter 1:19). Peter was referring to the prophecies that pointed to Christ (cf. 2 Peter 1:16). We not only have the prophecies; we also have their fulfillment in Christ. Jesus affirmed that "all the things which are written about [Him] in the Law of Moses and the Prophets and the Psalms must be fulfilled" (Luke 24:44-46), and was fulfilled. As a "lamp shining in a dark place," these prophecies revealed the mystery that was otherwise unknowable but has been revealed by the Spirit (1 Corinthians 2:11-12).

To ourselves – "Pay close attention to yourself...for as you do this you will ensure salvation...for yourself..." (1 Timothy 4:16). This is about our conduct and our standing before God. Paul told the Corinthians, "Test yourselves to see if you are in the faith; examine yourselves!" (2 Corinthians 13:5). We need to do the same thing. We will "all appear before the judgment seat of Christ, so that each one may be recompensed for his deeds in the body, according to what he has done, whether good or bad" (2 Corinthians 5:10). We do not want to be surprised on that day and find out that we have not been serving the Lord as faithfully as we should (cf. Matthew 7:22-23).

To our teaching – "Pay close attention to yourself and to your teaching; persevere in these things, for as you do this you will ensure salvation both for yourself and for those who hear you" (1 Timothy 4:16). These are the things that we teach to others. Whenever we speak on spiritual matters – those things that have been revealed in the Scriptures – we have an obligation to "speak as the oracles of God" (1 Peter 4:11, KJV). Paul told Timothy, "Retain the standard of sound words which you have heard from me, in the faith and love which are in Christ Jesus" (2 Timothy 1:13). As we noticed earlier, we must not teach anything contrary to this (Galatians 1:8-9).

Don't Pay Attention to These Things

Myths – "Nor pay attention to myths...which give rise to mere speculation rather than furthering the administration of God which is by faith" (1 Timothy 1:4; cf. Titus 1:14). Myths are typically not true, but are carefully crafted in order to make a point. Peter wrote, "For we did not follow cleverly devised tales when we made known to you the power and coming of our Lord Jesus Christ, but were eyewitnesses of His majesty" (2 Peter 1:16). We need to avoid such myths because we are to follow the truth, not just anything that sounds right. Paul warned of false teachers who would deceive others "by their smooth and flattering speech" (Romans 16:17-18). Just because something sounds good does not mean it is right.

Endless genealogies – "Nor pay attention to...endless genealogies which give rise to mere speculation rather than furthering the administration of God which is by faith" (1 Timothy 1:4). Paul was not referring to inspired genealogies (cf. Matthew 1:1-17; Luke 3:23-38); instead, he was talking about records that go on indefinitely for no purpose. He said they are to be avoided because they were unprovable ("speculation") and ultimately meaningless. John the Baptist rebuked the Pharisees and Sadducees who would have trusted in their "endless genealogies" when he said, "Do not suppose that you can say to yourselves, 'We have Abraham for our father'; for I say to you that from these stones God is able to raise up children to Abraham" (Matthew 3:9). Paul explained to the Galatians that regardless of whether we are Jews or Gentiles, if "we belong to Christ," we are "Abraham's descendants, heirs according to promise" (Galatians 3:28-29). Our physical lineage does not impact our standing before God.

Deceitful spirits – "But the Spirit explicitly says that in later times some will fall away from the faith, paying attention to deceitful spirits..." (1 Timothy 4:1). These are those who would lead us away from the faith through deception. Paul warned, "For such men are false apostles, deceitful workers, disguising themselves as apostles of Christ. No wonder, for even Satan disguises himself as an angel of light.

Therefore, it is not surprising if his servants also disguise themselves as servants of righteousness, whose end will be according to their deeds" (2 Corinthians 11:13-15). While God is not fooled by these false teachers, many people are. We need to avoid them because they can cause us to "fall away from the faith" which means we will be lost. We must "be faithful until death" and "hold fast the beginning of our assurance firm until the end" if we want to be saved (Revelation 2:10; Hebrews 3:14).

Doctrines of demons – "But the Spirit explicitly says that in later times some will fall away from the faith, paying attention to...doctrines of demons" (1 Timothy 4:1). These are teachings that contradict the doctrine of Christ. In giving the Great Commission, Jesus told His apostles, "Go therefore and make disciples of all the nations, baptizing them in the name of the Father and the Son and the Holy Spirit, teaching them to observe all that I commanded you" (Matthew 28:19-20). We are to obey the Lord's commands, but those who promote the "doctrines of demons" want us to follow something different. We must avoid them because they will cause us to lose our fellowship with God. John warned about this: "Anyone who goes too far and does not abide in the teaching of Christ, does not have God; the one who abides in the teaching, he has both the Father and the Son" (2 John 9). Having or not having God is about fellowship. By following teachings that contradict the gospel, we no longer have fellowship with God

Commandments of men – "Not paying attention to... commandments of men who turn away from the truth" (Titus 1:14). This was a warning against following man-made rules in the realm of religion. This was like the Pharisees and scribes who criticized Jesus' disciples for breaking "the tradition of the elders" by "not [washing] their hands when they eat bread" (Matthew 15:2). These man-made rules need to be avoided because following them does not help our service to God. Paul described such rules as having "the appearance of wisdom in self-made religion," but were "of no value against fleshly indulgence" (Colossians 2:23). In quoting the prophet Isaiah, Jesus plainly said, "But in vain do they worship Me, teaching as doctrines the precepts of men" (Matthew 15:9). No matter how much these rules "make sense" to us, following them as a matter of faith is actually detrimental to our fellowship with God.

Why This Matters

Our attention affects our direction – If we pay attention to "deceitful spirits and doctrines of demons," we will "fall away from the faith" (1 Timothy 4:1). If we do not pay attention "to what we have heard" in the gospel, we will "drift away from it" (Hebrews 2:1). Jesus said that we are to follow the straight and narrow path (Matthew 7:13-14). Paul emphasized the need for us to "press on toward the goal" of heaven (Philippians 3:14). We cannot stay on the right path and reach our goal if we are not paying attention to the direction we are going.

Our attention affects our understanding – Peter said we are to "pay attention" to the word because it is as "a lamp shining in a dark place" (2 Peter 1:19). In other words, we can gain enlightenment or understanding as we pay attention to the inspired word of God. Paul said we are to "understand what the will of the Lord is" (Ephesians 5:17). The only way we can do this is by giving attention to the study of the Scriptures. This is why he told Timothy, "Be diligent to present yourself approved to God as a workman who does not need to be ashamed, accurately handling the word of truth" (2 Timothy 2:15).

Our attention affects our service to God– When Paul warned about paying attention to "myths and endless genealogies," he said that doing so would hinder our ability to help in "furthering the administration of God which is by faith" (1 Timothy 1:4). This is about building up and contributing to the work of God. Paul admonished the brethren in Corinth, "Therefore, my beloved brethren, be steadfast, immovable, always abounding in the work of the Lord, knowing that your toil is not in vain in the Lord" (1 Corinthians 15:58). As members of the church, the work of each one of us "causes the growth of the body for the building up of itself in love" (Ephesians 4:16). We have to pay attention to the right things in order to serve God as He wants us to serve Him.

Our attention affects our salvation (and that of others) – Paul told Timothy, "Pay close attention to yourself and to your teaching" because this would "ensure salvation both for yourself and for those who hear you" (1 Timothy 4:16). The gospel is "the power of God for salvation to everyone who believes" (Romans 1:16) and Jesus is "to all those who obey Him the source of eternal salvation" (Hebrews 5:9). We must believe and obey the gospel to be saved. Therefore, we need to pay attention to what it teaches and instructs us to do.

Conclusion

If we understand that our eternal destiny is important, then we need to pay attention to what the word of God says, pay attention to ourselves to make sure we live up to His standard, and avoid being distracted by those things that are contrary to God's will. Let us always be willing to take time to consider whether our focus is where it needs to be.

Proverbs 2: Value of Wisdom June 14, 2020 We continue our study of Proverbs with Chapter 2. The first few words reflect what we saw in the "introductory" chapter, in 1:8 "Hear, my son, your Father's instructions, and reject not your mother's teachings; ..." Notice "hear," not "read." In antiquity, it was expected that words of wisdom would be delivered spoken. Indeed, ancient systems of writing were more of a way to keep records and remind a speaker what to say. Even in New Testament times, Greek was written in a style called "Biblical Unical," that is, all capital letters, with no spaces between words, and no punctuation. That makes it difficult to read, at least the first time. But typically, the reader was saying the words aloud, very familiar words, and only needed to glance at what was written occasionally. Paul's letters, even, were not meant to be circulated and read silently among members of a congregation, but to be read aloud, by a message bearer, who was familiar with the contents. Hebrew, in antiquity, not only omitted spaces between words and punctuation, but also the vowels. So the reader needed to be quite familiar with the language; one needed to decode the (typically) three letter codes for words and know how to pronounce them. Have you ever stopped to marvel at language and speech and reading We take these things for granted? Children learn these things without our really understanding how. Yes, we do try to "school" them in reading. Getting a bit of instruction for that helps. But the rest is a marvel beyond understanding, that starts with children hearing their parents' voices. By the time they are five or six years old, they are amazingly proficient. So, why is it that they need another dozen or so years to be considered "adults" We know why; there is still much to learn! Much that a child of five or six, just starting school, can't yet comprehend. So, here's where the book of Proverbs comes in. As best I understand it, after the exile, the collection of Proverbs, credited to Solomon and various other wise men, was organized as we have it. It seems to have served as something of a textbook, specifically for young men approaching adulthood. These words of wisdom would have been spoken. The reader was likely not literally the young man's father, but a "wise man" given the responsibility of further preparing the young men of a community, very likely the local rabbi. (Unlike our own younger years, after the printing press had been invented, written material was precious and uncommon. Students would not have had their own copies, as we did our textbooks. The teacher would convey this wisdom by reading it aloud.) 2 Now, make no mistake; "wisdom" was not the sole preserve of men, as some might extrapolate from the "father to son" language of Proverbs. Indeed, the first people titled as "wise" in the Bible are two women, unnamed, but obviously important, in II Samuel 14 (the wise woman of Tekoa) and 20:14 ff. (the wise woman of Bethmaacah). It may well be that a leading "wise woman" was an important office in at least some cities of the time. Similarly, the first named prophet in the Bible is Moses's sister Miriam, who saw the events at the Red Sea and proclaimed that this was God's work. We know about the importance of Deborah during the time of the Judges. By the time the Proverbs collection was edited into its current form, young women would have been expected to learn from their mothers, just as young men from their fathers. But this extra step of more formal instruction that we are reading was reserved for, and tailored for, just the young men. Proverbs Chapter 2 is all one long poem. Indeed, grammatically, it is all one sentence! Do you recall diagramming sentences back in high school or junior high We almost need to do that to follow the structure of this chapter? (Our NRSV translation puts a period at the end of verse 11. The RSV puts a semicolon there, and KJV puts a colon.) The overall structure is: If (verses 1-4 – seek and receive wisdom) Then (verses 5-8 - first of five blessings: knowledge of God) Then (verses 9-11 – second blessing: live ordered by wisdom) (Then implied) (verses 12-15 – third blessing: protection from evil men) (Then implied) (verses 16-19 – fourth blessing: protection from evil women) (So–then implied) (verses 20-22 – fifth blessing: for those who walk in wisdom) Verses 1 and 2 distinguish teachings of wisdom from teachings of the Law. ".. if you receive my words …" The wise man is speaking his own words of wisdom, and so, in a sense, with his own authority. This is a marked contrast to the words of a prophet, who speaks saying, "Thus saith the LORD, …." By Jesus's time, the written scripture (the Law and the Prophets), as well as written words in The Writings (such as Proverbs and Psalms), played a much more important role. Proverbs was a written book; the teacher would be depending on his source as an authority, not as much his own meditations or thoughts. Even the spoken Law enforced by the Pharisees was based on tradition. Student Pharisees such as the young Saul would have learned from their teachers what wise men of old had said, and would have depended on being able to quote such "authorities" in their discourse. Much like scholarship in our day. 3 That's why Jesus's teaching was so revolutionary. At the conclusion of "The Sermon on the Mount," in Matthew 7:28, we read: Now when Jesus had finished saying these things [his teachings in Matt 5-7], the crowds were astounded at his teaching, for he taught as one having authority, and not as their scribes. People of Jesus's day were used to teaching always referencing sources and citations. Jesus WAS an authority, not just a learned source of quotes. Getting back to Proverbs 2: Verses 2 - 5 make clear that it's not enough just to "hear". We need to "listen", "be attentive", "seek" and "search". We hear lots of stuff that we don't ever notice. For example, Cindy and I live right off of Wyoming Avenue. There is traffic. There is a traffic signal where trucks and other vehicles screech to a stop and loudly accelerate on the green. Often I hear it. Occasionally I even notice it. When we have had company stay with us, though, it can be disturbing to them. For us, not noticing it is helpful. It is just noise with little or no meaning. But, let us not get so used to hearing God's word, or words of wisdom, that we let it wash over us without listening! Do you recall being in school and just not paying attention at all to what was being taught I can. Such teaching did not do me any good. In some cases, I rationalized that I didn't need to listen. In many of those, and other cases, I certainly should have! I wasted time, and threw away a teacher's efforts. The writer of this poem is telling us to take advantage of the opportunity. These words are a gift, a blessing, that we should pursue diligently. The first blessing is that, for those who listen and are upright, they receive "sound wisdom" that comes from God. The term translated as "sound wisdom" is unusual, found outside Job and proverbs only in Isaiah 28:29 and Micah 6:9. The word seems to imply deliverance or protection, seen in the rest of this passage: "he is a shield... guarding the paths of justice and preserving the way of his saints." The second blessing is understanding righteousness, justice, equity, and "every good path." The effects are "pleasant." This may seem odd. But, consider: doesn't understanding what is going on help us make sense of our circumstances in ways that can make the difficult bearable as a child, I was on one occasion being taken to the doctor's office to get a "shot". I was perhaps four or five, and I knew what a "shot" was. I didn't understand though. I declared, "I hope we come to a hundred traffic lights, and they are all red!" After the shot had been delivered, I said, "Was that all" The fear and dread of the shot was much worse than the shot itself. As an adult, my perspective is different. I can take pleasure while waiting 4 outside a theater, for example, knowing that the concert or show is worth the wait. If it's a familiar one, I can in my mind hear or see scenes I can anticipate as I wait, or take pleasure in conversation about it. Understanding allows us to make more sense of the world we live in, the bad as well as the good. If we can but just have faith that God can use the happenings of our world for His purposes, we can perhaps detach ourselves from fear, and avoid pitfalls, by being "discerning." The third blessing, 12-15, is specifically protection from evil men. As I read these lines, what comes to my mind are the kinds of evil juvenile boys dream up and like to talk about. I'm sort of put back into the days of my own youth. In the "Christmas Story" movie, the protagonist Ralphie says that there are only "bullies, toadies, and victims." In the movie, the bully and toady are outside his closer world of family and classroom. The bully is a hazard going and coming to school. But probably more commonly, bullying is a part of life for a young boy, even within the classroom (and recess), even within the Sunday school class, possibly within the scout troop, and perhaps within the family. The words of verse 14 ring true: "Who rejoice in doing evil and delight in perverseness of evil." That's the dominant male in the peer group, who coerces others to follows his ways, or be turned into a victim. The result: not only petty crimes, but the use of power to bring others into those crimes as well. These verses may sound different to women. They have their own social problems growing up, and I doubt they are any less stressful than what boys experience. Probably worse. I can't speak to that. I know it's just as real. The fourth blessing of wisdom is protection from wicked women. Proverbs paints a more detailed picture of this hazard in 7:6-27. I give thanks that I can't speak to this particular with any authority myself, but the hazard is real. Again, this is wisdom specifically to young men. You women can surely describe just as vividly the peril to young women, no less real, and, if anything, even more dangerous. The lesson book lists Genesis 39 as also being a scripture for this week. That's the story of Joseph and Potiphar's wife. It's a specific illustration of this issue. Even though in the short run Joseph is the one who is hurt (and put in jail), ultimately God uses that event as a means of saving both Egypt and his own people. The concluding blessing is a summary. It promises good to the righteous. "For the upright will inhabit the land. And men of integrity will remain in it;" And destruction to the wicked. 5 To me, this passage also speaks a word of reassurance. We are not alone. There are others remaining, also, who walk in righteousness. I am reminded of the prophet Elijah, threatened by Jezebel, who fled to Mount Horeb, the mountain of God. God asked, "What are you doing here, Elijah" Elijah answered, "…. the Israelites have forsaken your covenant, thrown down your altars, and killed your prophets with the sword. I alone am left, and they are seeking my life, to take it away." (1 Kings 19: 10) Elijah sees himself as standing completely alone, and seeks refuge where God may be found. But God ultimately tells him, "Yet I will leave seven thousand in Israel, all the knees that have not bowed to Baal, and every mouth that has not kissed him." (v 18). Elijah is NOT left alone. There remain many faithful, thousands. In his zealousness and focus, Elijah could not see them. The same is true for us sometimes. There are many good and faithful people in this world. They are not always apparent. In times like these, with the epidemic and its consequences causing havoc, sometimes it is easier to see, to discern, those good people. For example, in the person of doctors and nurses, and others, who are faithful to their calling to help others despite the danger. We need to give thanks to God for those, and for all of God's many saints among us. We are not alone.

One of Jesus's most repeated sayings in the Gospels is some version of this: "If anyone has ears to hear, let him hear" (Mark 4:23). If we're wise, we'll listen carefully to whatever Jesus says, especially what he says repeatedly. And in this case, listening happens to be precisely what he's telling us to do.

There's a very, very important reason behind Jesus's exhortation:

"Pay attention to what you hear: with the measure you use, it will be measured to you, and still more will be added to you. For to the one who has, more will be given, and from the one who has not, even what he has will be taken away." (Mark 4:24–25)

Do you understand what Jesus is saying The fact that this warning itself is somewhat difficult to understand illustrates his point: listen and ponder carefully, for if you don't, you will not understand, and if you do not understand, you will lose whatever capacity to understand you do have.

Everything hangs on how well you hear what God is saying — what we commonly call the word of God. And hearing God well requires your close attention. Are you paying attention

The Strange Purpose of Parables

Jesus issues this warning in the context of telling a series of parables. Parables were riddle-stories in which Jesus hid profound secrets of God's kingdom in brief, often mundane-sounding metaphors.

In the stories recorded in Mark 4, he uses a farmer's soils (Mark 4:1–8), an oil lamp (Mark 4:21–25), and seeds (Mark 4:26–32).

Read them. Do you understand them Of course; Jesus explains the parable of the soils (Mark 4:13–20). But what about the lamp or the seeds These stories sound simpler than they are. We won't really get them unless we are paying attention.

And we have Bibles! None of Jesus's original hearers had ever heard these parables before. They weren't written down so they could be read over and over, have their grammatical structure examined, and be conveniently cross-referenced with other Scriptures. The first hearers heard these stories once. If they weren't paying attention, they would miss the kingdom. That's costly distraction.

When Jesus explained to his disciples why he taught in parables, he said he did so — quoting portions of Isaiah 6:9–10 — that his hearers "may indeed see but not perceive, and may indeed hear but not understand, lest they should turn and be forgiven" (Mark 4:12). Here again, Jesus's hard-to-understand explanation illustrates his point: if we're not listening carefully, we'll miss what he's saying.

Is God really telling riddles so that people won't understand No and yes. Jesus told the parables to reveal spiritual mysteries of the kingdom, and he really wanted people to understand them. That's why he said, "If anyone has ears to hear, let him hear" and "Pay attention." But his revelatory method tested the spiritual wakefulness and earnestness of the hearers. Those who were listening to really hear would hear. But the spiritually dull and distracted would not. Jesus wanted to give the kingdom to the former, not the latter. Those who would not pay attention would reveal their spiritual dullness — dullness that has serious consequences: missing the kingdom of God.

God's Counterintuitive Ways

If Jesus's words here sound counterintuitive, they are. Jesus spoke and acted in ways consistent with God's words and ways throughout the Bible, captured in this text:

"For my thoughts are not your thoughts, neither are your ways my ways, declares the Lord. For as the heavens are higher than the earth, so are my ways higher than your ways and my thoughts than your thoughts." (Isaiah 55:8–9)

I've seen this passage, or some portion of it, quoted on Christian memes, calendars, and greeting cards, often with a beautiful inspirational landscape, seascape, or skyscraper in the background. But if we inserted biblical images as backgrounds, they'd be things like a forbidden tree in Eden, the existence of Satan, a horrific flood, Abraham about to sacrifice Isaac, Jacob disguised as Esau, Joseph languishing in prison, Israel with a sea before them and the Egyptian army behind them, Rahab the Canaanite prostitute marrying into the messianic bloodline, David hiding in a cave from Saul, Jeremiah weeping over

Jewish women boiling their babies, baby Jesus sleeping in a trough, and above all, adult Jesus mutilated and hanging on a Roman cross.

God's ways truly are not our ways. None of us would have written the story of redemption the way God has. The story itself points to a Personality and intentionality behind it.

And if we're paying attention, we can detect the same Personality and intentionality in the strange way Jesus communicates the kingdom of God in hard-to-understand parables. None of us would do it that way.

Familiar, Affluent, and Distracted

The key qualifier is if we're paying attention. Because, as Jesus said, if we're not paying attention to what God says, we will miss what God is doing. That's a costly distraction.

By God's grace, we do have an advantage over Jesus's original hearers: we have God's authoritative, written word. In fact, never have so many Christians had so much access to God's word as we do today.

But we must not be lulled into thinking that so much access to and familiarity with Jesus's teaching means we don't face the same danger as those first-century listeners. We may have a clearer view of the kingdom than the crowds who heard Jesus's parables, but we are as endangered by dull hearing as anyone has ever been (Hebrews 5:11).

Never have Christians possessed so much wealth as Western Christians today, which presents many temptations to us and threatens to destroy us (1 Timothy 6:9–10). And never have Christians been barraged with so many and so varied distractions as we are. Overly familiar, overly affluent, and overly distracted is a recipe for the kind of dull hearing that often manifests as being able to explain what Jesus means without actually doing what he says.

It is a false comfort to be able to accurately teach a text if we do not obey it, if functionally our fleshly anxieties and desires govern us, not Jesus's commands and promises. This can be a more deceptive form of dull hearing than merely not listening or forgetting.

Pay Much Closer Attention

"Therefore we must pay much closer attention to what we have heard, lest we drift away from it" (Hebrews 2:1). If we're not paying attention, we may not even realize we're drifting. We can look around and see lots of other distracted, dull Christians who talk Jesus's talk without walking Jesus's walk, figure it must be normal, and assume we're doing just fine. The only way we know if we're paying close attention to what Jesus says, in the way that he means it, is if we are really doing what he says (John 14:15).

The Christian life is an attentive life (Mark 13:37; Luke 21:36; Ephesians 6:18; 1 Thessalonians 5:6; 1 Peter 5:8). The Christian life is a hearing life (Mark 4:24; Luke 8:21; John 10:27; Romans 10:17; Hebrews 3:7–8). But attentive listening to Jesus does not come naturally. It must be cultivated and diligently guarded. And there is no formula for how to pay closer attention. It is cultivated by making attentiveness habitual — by practicing the habits of grace. We learn to pay attention by intentionally trying to pay attention. The Spirit will help us if we ask the Father to teach us (Luke 11:9–10; Psalm 25:4).

So whatever it takes, we must pay attention to what we hear. For Jesus's ways and words are often counterintuitive, and we live in a destructively distracting age. And everything hangs on how well we hear Jesus.

So all of this that is being said adult children please take heed to what I'm saying pay attention to your parents and follow instruction and direction and you will live a better life and you would not have to depend on your parents as much because in reality we as parent don't owe you nothing but advice and how to get through this world and live a better life with the lords and your parents take this story and this moral and I hope you can understand

When you see pictures of gardens in magazines or advertisements, they always seem so clean and pristine. I must be doing something wrong because every year I grow a garden; it never looks like the ads. It's almost inevitable that I will have weeds. Not only that, but since the beginning, I've also had to deal with another culprit-bugs.

With the weeds, I've learned to identify a few recurring ones. Dandelions are pretty common. They have a carrot shaped root and if you try to pull it up, it's designed to allow the top to pop off while leaving the root. If they bloom enough to spread seeds, you'll have hundreds in a few weeks. The English Ivy is still trying to make a comeback. Some of the seeds are still in the soil. This plant shoots out and crawls along the ground. If you pull one out, it still has branches everywhere else. A surprising weed ended up being regular grass. The clippings from my lawn and some of the seeds used for reseeding the lawn got into my garden. They ended up growing and were really hard to pull out. There were also plenty of other weeds that I couldn't identify. At first, I didn't know which plant it was. I thought some of these plants were some of the plants I had planted earlier. But it turned out that a lot of these plants ended up being weeds.

Weeds are annoying because they competed with the plants I was trying to grow. They were harmful on numerous levels. Sometimes they choked the garden plants by wrapping around them, took much-needed nutrients, gobbled up space that would normally be for the garden plant, and blocked the sun if the weed grew big enough.

Here are some lessons I learned about weeds. First, the thing with weed plants is that it isn't enough to clear it once. I had to go back to it after a few weeks. It meant that the garden needed constant tending. If I went on a mission trip or a vacation, it was not uncommon for me to find that the garden plants to have grown, but I also found the weeds did too.

Second, it's easier to pull up the plants when the plants are young and if the ground is soft after some rain. If the plant grew up it took up more soil and the roots ran deeper. If it grew next to other plants, the root systems got entwined. If I were to pull up the weed, I risked pulling up the good plants as well.

The second issue I had to deal with were the insects. Dealing with a garden, particularly an organic garden required being watchful over bugs that apparently eat fruit and vegetables more than my kids do.

In the spring, before it gets too warm, the primary bug of concern is this kind of small gnat that jumps around and that turns into a fly. Later on, green translucent bugs come on the scene called aphids start laying eggs and hiding under the leaves of tomato and eggplant leaves. Last year I also growing strawberries and found little holes and tunnels in my strawberries. The culprit Slugs.

I was introduced to a world of organic pesticides. Soap water is very effective on bugs. Apparently, it dries out the bugs and keeps them from flying off. I had to regularly spray under the leaves and find them out. I also came across a very interesting remedy for slugs: beer. Apparently, they are attracted to the smell of fermentation. I found out a small container of beer will attract a lot of slugs. They eventually fall into it and drown.

It isn't too hard to find spiritual analogies in these situations. Growing weeds and finding pests that threaten a garden is not difficult to find. All it takes is for a gardener to let the garden go. Similarly, spiritually, if we are not paying attention, or watching out for our spiritual state, we can allow weeds and pests to wreak havoc on our relationship with God.

Paul writes in Romans 13:11–12, "Besides this you know the time, that the hour has come for you to wake from sleep. For salvation is nearer to us now than when we first believed. The night is far gone; the day is at hand. So then let us cast off the works of darkness and put on the armor of light." (ESV) We need to be alert in our faith. We are called to watch out and not allow things to develop in our lives before they can get too big.

What are some things we need to watch out for Perhaps it might be a flirtatious conversation that can eventually lead to adultery? What about dinner with an old boyfriend or girlfriend for teenagers, it may be a word of sarcasm that hides pride. Perhaps an attitude of annoyance with parents that if left unaddressed could turn into rebellion against God's authority. All these things are things that too can consume the garden of our faith if we are not careful in dealing with these problems early on. They slowly erode our sense of humility and our sense of need for God. May the Lord give us wisdom and diligence to watch out for these seeds that can turn problems.

This message aims to describe for children what wisdom means and where it comes from. Young people might think of wisdom as mere knowledge or "head smarts", but true wisdom comes from the heart. Wisdom is something that we should desire because God wants us to have it and practice using it. The message uses practical objects and misconceptions to elaborate on what wisdom is. God wants us to act as wise and not foolish people. However, He gives us the tools to do so, if only we ask. True wisdom comes from recognizing that all we have comes from the Lord, and that who we are is found in Christ. We are not wise because we know a lot of book information or because we think we're better than others. We can be wise because Jesus lives in us. He promises His presence, and when we read God's word and pray, we can discern wise choices for our lives.

Solomon loved the Lord, walking in the statutes of David his father, only he sacrificed and made offerings at the high places. 4 And the king went to Gibeon to sacrifice there, for that was the great high place. Solomon used to offer a thousand burnt offerings on that altar. 5 At Gibeon the Lord appeared to Solomon in a dream by night, and God said, "Ask what I shall give you." 6 And Solomon said, "You have shown great and steadfast love to your servant David my father, because he walked before you in faithfulness, in righteousness, and in uprightness of heart toward you. And you have kept for him this great and steadfast love and have given him a son to sit on his throne this day. 7 And now, O Lord my God, you have made your servant king in place of David my father, although I am but a little child. I do not know how to go out or come in. 8 And your servant is in the midst of your people whom you have chosen, a great people, too many to be numbered or counted for multitude. 9 Give your servant therefore an understanding mind to govern your people, that I may discern between good and evil, for who is able to govern this your great people"

10 It pleased the Lord that Solomon had asked this. 11 And God said to him, "Because you have asked this, and have not asked for yourself long life or riches or the life of your enemies, but have asked for yourself understanding to discern what is right, 12 behold, I now do according to your word. Behold, I give you a wise and discerning mind, so that none like you has been before you and none like you shall arise after you. 13 I give you also what you have not asked, both riches and honor, so that no other king shall compare with you, all your days. 14 And if you will walk in my ways, keeping my statutes and my commandments, as your father David walked, then I will lengthen your days.". -1 Kings 3:3-14

Look carefully then how you walk, not as unwise but as wise, 16 making the best use of the time, because the days are evil. 17 Therefore do not be foolish, but understand what the will of the Lord is. 18 And do not get drunk with wine, for that is debauchery, but be filled with the Spirit, 19 addressing one another in psalms and hymns and spiritual songs, singing and making melody to the Lord with your heart, 20 giving thanks always and for everything to God the Father in the name of our Lord Jesus Christ, 21 submitting to one another out of reverence for Christ.   -Ephesians 5:15-21

Wisdom is a precious commodity that seems in awfully short supply today. And that's a shame because the Bible says few things are more important than possessing wisdom. In Proverbs 3 God says about wisdom. Let's read it together. "Happy is the person who becomes wise, who come to have understanding. There is more profit in it than there is in gold or silver; it is worth more to you than gold. Wisdom is more valuable to you than jewels; nothing you could want can compare to it!" So just what is wisdom Somebody once said this about wisdom. "Everybody is a fool at least five minutes a day. Wisdom consists in not exceeding that limit." That's one definition. But here is a better one, one that's more Biblical. You have it on your outline. Wisdom is the Spirit-given ability to see with discernment and to view life as God perceives it. True wisdom does not view life just with the five senses, what we see, touch, hear, taste, and smell. True wisdom views life the way God sees it with the sixth sense of faith. Wisdom is the Spirit-given ability to see with discernment and to view life as God perceives it. Now when you think of wisdom Solomon comes to mind. The Bible says Solomon was the wisest person who has ever lived. Now where did he get that wisdom in I King's 3 we read he acquired it through a prayer he prayed. His prayer is one of the great prayers of the Bible we are looking at in this message series. It's truly a difference making prayer. Last week we looked at a prayer of David when you need forgiveness. Today we're looking at Solomon's prayer when you need wisdom. As we look at this prayer there are four things God wants us to know about wisdom. I. First of all, God wants us to learn the need for wisdom. (Vs. 1-3) In these verses we see that Solomon loved the Lord and was trying to walk with God, and yet at the same time Solomon was still dong some foolish things. Two foolish things stand out. One: Solomon married a foreign wife, the daughter of Pharaoh as part of a political alliance. God had told his people they were not to enter into marriage with other nations, people who did not know the Lord. Secondly we read that Solomon was offering sacrifices on the high places. This was directly counter to God's Word given to his people when they entered the promise land. The high places were where pagan gods had been worshiped. God wanted his people to worship where he designated. Solomon did not do that. Yes, he loved the Lord; he walked according to the statues of his father David. But he was acting foolishly. He needed wisdom. We too need wisdom because we all can relate to Solomon. We love the Lord, but we act foolishly at times. There are times we say or think why did I do that There's the story of a little boy in a Children's Hospital as a patient. He was a terror and wreaking havoc with the nursing staff. He was visited by a man who knew the boy's reputation. He told the boy he would be back in a week and if this little boy behaved himself for a whole week he'd give him a dime. A week later the man came back and walked to the boys bed and said, "I'm not asking the nurses or staff about your behavior this past week, I just want you to tell me do you deserve the that dime. The little boy thought for a moment, looked at the man and said, give me a penny. That's what we would have to say isn't it. Yes, we know and love the Lord and want to live for him and yet just sometimes we act foolishly. This is the need for wisdom and we all have it. II. That's why after the need for wisdom, the next thing God wants us to learn is the nature of wisdom found in verses 4 and 5. God appears to Solomon in a dream and told him to ask for anything he wanted and it would be given to him. There's an offer you couldn't refuse. What if God come to each of us saying ask whatever you want and you will get it. What would we ask for; money, a bigger house, new car, better job, a decent boy or girl friend, better health, a longer vacation, or a more fulfilling retirement. Solomon did not ask for any of these things; instead he asked for one thing-wisdom. Why He knew the nature of wisdom; true wisdom, comes from God. True wisdom is found in the true God and Savior, Jesus Christ. This is what the Apostle Paul wrote to the early Christians. He said in Colossians chapter 2 "my purpose is that they (followers of Jesus) may be encouraged in heart and united in love, so that they may have the full riches of complete understanding, in order that they may know the mystery of God, namely, Christ, in whom are hidden all the treasures of wisdom and knowledge." Real wisdom, the kind of wisdom we need so much for our life, is found in God and the only way we can have it is through Jesus Christ and his work on the cross. Real wisdom is found in Jesus Christ and our having a relationship with him. In him are found all the treasure of wisdom and knowledge. We live in a world that looks for wisdom from scholars, philosophies, technology, society, our own reason, and from culture. And yet this is what the God says in I Corinthians 1 "For the message of the cross is foolishness to those who are perishing, but to us who are being saved it is the power of God. For it is written: I will destroy the wisdom of the wise; the intelligence of the intelligent I will frustrate. Where is the wise man Where is the scholar Where is the philosopher of the age Has Not God made foolish the wisdom of the world" This is the nature of wisdom. Wisdom comes from God and therefore if we are ever going to possess wisdom, we must learn to hear from God. God strives to get our attention because he wants us to hear from him because then and only then will we really possess true wisdom. III. That's why in this prayer after we see the need for wisdom and the nature of wisdom, we see the way to wisdom in verses 6-14. So what's the way to wisdom, the way to hear from God.

Well, it takes more than just right ears, it takes a right heart. We see three characteristic in Solomon's heart and God wants it in our heart too so we too can hear from God. So let's do a heart checkup. A. A heart that hears from God will be a heart of certainty we see in verse 6. A certain heart is a heart of faith. Solomon had a certainty that he was going to hear from God. Why Because he had a faith that God was loving, kind, and who was interested in him, thinking about him, and committed to guide him. (Read verse 6) Without a doubt Solomon had a heart of certainty and he would hear from God. And where do you think he got this kind of heart It is the same place our children will get a heart for God. It will be the power of the Holy Spirit working through our life and example. Solomon got his form his father David and look at what David wrote in Psalm 139 "How precious to me are your thoughts, O God! How vast is the sum of them! Were I to count them, they would outnumber the grains of sand. When I awake, I am still with you." It's the same for us. God loves us, is concerned for us, always thinking about us. His heart is continually toward us. He's committed to guide us. Like David we say how precious your thoughts, O God are. If I were to number them they would outnumber the grains of sand. There is a blood stained cross that proves God's love to us. It says God loves us so much he came to this earth and on the cross Jesus took upon himself the dilemma of our sin that separated us from God so we could know in a real way God's love. He did it not because we deserved it, but out of love for us. That's what makes us right with God and gives us a heart of certainty that enables us to hear from him. B. To hear from God, we also need a heart of humility which we see in Solomon in verse 7. (Read verse 7) Solomon could have thought I have everything under control. I snap my fingers and people jump. Instead Solomon says he is only a child and not sure what to do.

That's a heart of humility and that kind of heart will enable us to hear from God. Has God done anything in your life to help you to be more humble so you would be more open to hear from him A pastor was at the door greeting people as they left. One lady said, thanks pastor for that message. I really enjoyed it. The pastor replied don't thank me, thank the Lord. The woman said well it wasn't that good. God works allowing situations and circumstances in our life to humble us. Why It opens us up to hear God's voice. C. A heart of certainty, a heart of humility, and the third characteristic we see in Solomon is a heart of availability which we see in verses 8 and 9. This kind of heart too will enable us to hear from God. Solomon said God your servant is here. Solomon had more interest in serving, then being served; more interest in commitment than comfort; more interest in fulfilling the purpose of God, than fulfilling his own purpose. Would that be our description A heart of availability says God you speak to me and when you speak to me I'll do it. I'm willing, ready, and available. I'll do it; not just think about it. That's the kind of heart that hears from God. When you realize how loving Godin your Savior Jesus Christ is toward you; how concerned he is about you; how he knows more about you and what you need, than you'll ever know about yourself, you can do what God tells us to do. Why When you come to know that love that surpasses all knowledge, the grip of fear is broken and we can go forward in God. So like Solomon have a heart of availability. In this prayer we see God will speak to a heart of certainty, a heart of humility, and a heart of availability. God is speaking to us, are we hearing him. How does God speak to us today You have it in your outline? Follow along: How God Speaks Today: 1. The Word of God: so meditate upon Scripture! 2. The Counsel of others: so connect with mature Christian (ministry teams, small groups, ministry committees, etc.) 3. The circumstances of life: so ask "God what are you saying to me here" 4. The impressions of the Holy Spirit: So listen carefully for Him! God's Voice Will: 1. Consistent with the Word of God(Bible) 2. Conflict with natural wisdom 3. Clash with your sinful nature (I don't want to do that) 4. Challenge your faith 5. Call you to courage Hearing the voice of God takes practice. It's an acquired skill that comes the more you listen to God who works in you a heart of certainty, humility, and availability. And in that way you will have wisdom from on high. That's what happened to Solomon. We see it in verses 10-14. He got the wisdom he needed and along with that he received all the other stuff he didn't ask for. God is saying to us today other stuff will never fulfill your life. Make sure your priorities are in order; seek wisdom by seeking after a heart of certainty, humility, and availability. Why IV. After we see the need, the nature, and the way, we see the result of wisdom in verse 15. And what do we see in Solomon; worshipful obedience to God. Solomon left the high places and worshiped God the way and in the place God wanted to be worshiped. God not only confirmed his truth to Solomon, but he also conformed Solomon to his truth. And God will do the same thing in our life if we will seek him with a heart of certainty, humility, and availability. We will hear from him as he speaks to us confirming his truth to us and conforming us to his truth. Conclusion Yes wisdom is a precious commodity that seems in short supply today. But it does not need to be that way for the people of who love Jesus and follow Jesus. Because in Jesus are hidden all the treasures of wisdom and knowledge. If we embrace him by faith with a heart of growing certainty, with a heart of growing humility, and with a heart of growing availability God will not only confirm his truth to us, he will conform us to his truth. Why When everything is said and done I believe this prayer of Solomon is truly one of the greatest prayers of the Bible

During the darkest part of the night, who do you blame

Everything you want in life has a price connected to it. There's a price to pay if you want to make things better, a price to pay just for leaving things as they are, a price for everything."

I have the usual problem of deciding what to give you. I know you might enjoy many things — books, games, clothes.

I want to give you something that will stay with you for more than a few months or years. I want to give you a gift that might remind you of me every year around

If I could give you just one thing, I'd want it to be a simple truth that took me many years to learn. If you learn it now, it may enrich your life in hundreds of ways. And it may prevent you from facing many problems that have hurt people who have never learned it.

The truth is simply this: No one owes you anything.

Significance

How could such a simple statement be important It may not seem so, but understanding it can bless your entire life.

No one owes you anything.

It means that no one else is living for you, my child. Because no one is you. Each person is living for himself; his own happiness is all he can ever personally feel.

When you realize that no one owes you happiness or anything else, you'll be freed from expecting what isn't likely to be.

It means no one has to love you. If someone loves you, it's

because there's something special about you that gives him happiness. Find out what that something special is and try to make it stronger in you, so that you'll be loved even more.

When people do things for you, it's because they want to — because you, in some way, give them something meaningful that makes them want to please you, not because anyone owes you anything.

No one has to like you. If your friends want to be with you, it's not out of duty. Find out what makes others happy so they'll want to be near you.

No one has to respect you. Some people may even be unkind to you. But once you realize that people don't have to be good to you, and may not be good to you, you'll learn to avoid those who would harm you. For you don't owe them anything either.

Living your Life

No one owes you anything.

You owe it to yourself to be the best person possible. Because if you are, others will want to be with you, want to provide you with the things you want in exchange for what you're giving to them.

Some people will choose not to be with you for reasons that have nothing to do with you. When that happens, look elsewhere for the relationships you want. Don't make someone else's problem your problem.

Once you learn that you must earn the love and respect of others, you'll never expect the impossible and you won't be disappointed. Others don't have to share their property with you, nor their feelings or thoughts.

If they do, it's because you've earned these things. And you have every reason to be proud of the love you receive, your friends' respect, the property you've earned. But don't ever take them for granted. If you do, you could lose them. They're not yours by right; you must always earn them.

My Experience

A great burden was lifted from my shoulders the day I realized that no one owes me anything. For so long as I'd thought there were things I was entitled to, I'd been wearing myself out —physically and emotionally — trying to collect them.

No one owes me moral conduct, respect, friendship, love, courtesy, or intelligence. And once I recognized that, all my relationships became far more satisfying. I've focused on being with people who want to do the things I want them to do.

That understanding has served me well with friends, business associates, lovers, sales prospects, and strangers. It constantly reminds me that I can get what I want only if I can enter the other person's world. I must try to understand how he thinks, what he believes to be important, what he wants. Only then can I appeal to someone in ways that will bring me what I want.

And only then can I tell whether I really want to be involved with someone. And I can save the important relationships for those with whom I have the most in common.

It's not easy to sum up in a few words what has taken me years to learn. But maybe if you re-read this gift each Christmas, the meaning will become a little clearer every year.

I hope so, for I want more than anything else for you to understand this simple truth that can set you free.

• I'm going to leave you with this

• In Ephesians 2:8:10 FATHER YOU KNOW THE AREAS WHERE MY CHILDREN ARE WEAK

SHAPE THEM THIS YEAR IN WAYS THAT COULD ONLY REFLECT YOUR POWER WORKING

IN AND AROUND THEM.

www.ingramcontent.com/pod-product-compliance
Lightning Source LLC
Chambersburg PA
CBHW051528120626
46551CB00012B/1123